LIBRARIES AND KEY PERFORMANCE INDICATORS

D1388844

LIBRARIES AND KEY PERFORMANCE INDICATORS

A Framework for Practitioners

LEO APPLETON

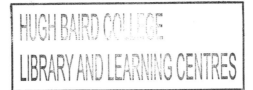

CHANDOS PUBLISHING

An imprint of Elsevier

Chandos Publishing is an imprint of Elsevier
50 Hampshire Street, 5th Floor, Cambridge, MA 02139, United States
The Boulevard, Langford Lane, Kidlington, OX5 1GB, United Kingdom

Library of Congress Cataloging-in-Publication Data
A catalog record for this book is available from the Library of Congress

British Library Cataloguing-in-Publication Data
A catalogue record for this book is available from the British Library

ISBN: 978-0-08-100227-8 (print)
ISBN: 978-0-08-100255-1 (online)

For information on all Chandos publications
visit our website at https://www.elsevier.com/books-and-journals

Publisher: Glyn Jones
Acquisition Editor: George Knott
Editorial Project Manager: Anna Valutkevich
Production Project Manager: Debasish Ghosh
Cover Designer: Greg Harris

Typeset by SPi Global, India

CONTENTS

ABOUT THE AUTHOR

Leo Appleton is the Director of Library Services at Goldsmiths, University of London where he is responsible for the operational and strategic management of the university's library services. His previous roles include Associate Director posts at the University of the Arts, London and Liverpool John Moores University and he has held library leadership and management positions in several other higher and further education institutions. During his professional career Leo has been involved in many aspects of library and information provision and management including academic liaison and support, library space and building design, quality assurance and performance measurement, staff development and training, technology enhanced learning, collection development, and the provision of electronic and digital library resources. He has presented and published widely on several of these areas.

Leo is a chartered fellow of the Chartered Institute of Library and Information Professionals and he is currently active within the Multimedia, Information and Technology group (MmIT), as the editor of the *MmIT Journal*. Leo is also the associate editor of the *New Review of Academics Librarianship* and co-editor of the UKSG electronic newsletter *eNews*. Leo also has a long standing and active involvement with SCONUL and is currently a member of its Transformation Group.

Leo's professional interests include performance measurement of libraries and strategic approaches to service delivery. He is currently studying for a PhD at Edinburgh Napier University in which he is investigating the value and impact of UK public libraries on citizenship development. This research is taking him outside of his natural higher education environment as he conducts his empirical research in public libraries across the United Kingdom.

CHAPTER ONE

Introduction

The idea for this book came from a workshop which was delivered at the 10th Northumbria International Conference on Performance Measurement in Libraries and Information Services, which took place in York in 2013. The workshop was delivered by myself and other colleagues from the SCONUL Performance Measurement and Quality Strategy Group, which had been tasked with looking at the value of the then existing SCONUL statistical return, which all UK university libraries are encouraged to return. This workshop, along with several other regional workshops that had been delivered at UK university libraries during 2013, and a survey sent out to all UK library directors, ultimately helped to inform the recommendations for a change in approach to the SCONUL statistical return. This is well documented in a chapter by Alison Mackenzie (2016) and details some of the thinking behind how we need to review our statistics and measures to keep them relevant, meaningful, and valuable. The epiphany moment for me, during the discussions at this workshop, was that many UK university librarians and library managers were referring to the SCONUL statistics as being their library's 'Key Performance Indicators' and were reporting them as such internally. This was and still is common practice and many library services (across all sectors) return their usage statistics both locally and within their sectors as being indicative of the performance. In many cases libraries tend to try to make their usage statistics fit into a set of performance indicators or key performance indicators (as this is what will have been requested) and this practice can be the cause of much deliberation, confusion, and anxiety.

To problematise this practice would be to acknowledge that library metrics and usage statistics are not performance indicators or key performance indicators and should therefore not be referred to as such. But it isn't as easy as this, and librarians are very proud of being able to demonstrate high levels of usage and value for money through their meticulously collected statistics and data. Often the parent organisation, within which the library sits, requests such usage data in order to hold the library to account or justify its funding or financial resources, so collection of statistics and metrics becomes even more important.

In recent years, there has also been an increase in the accountability of library services to their users and customers and subsequently the development of customer facing services standards (grounded in achievable but challenging targets) has become the norm for library services. These are of course another level of statistical reporting which sit within the broader theme of library performance measurement, and as with usage statistics are often referred to as performance indicators or KPIs. Again, as with usage statistics, customer service standards are not technically KPIs, although there is a strong argument that they are indicators of performance.

There are several attributes and characteristics of a true Key Performance Indicator (KPI) and they will be explored further during the course of this book, alongside other types of statistics and metrics which can be used to 'indicate performance'. The terms Key Performance Indicators and KPIs are used very liberally throughout the literature available on strategic management, and this is certainly reflected upon when looking at the current practices in the libraries. KPIs are usually alluded to when discussing performance measurement or quality assurance and are widely acknowledged as being a set of statistical measures that focus on the key areas of the business with regard to measuring and indicating (at a glance) how successful those key areas are at a particular moment in time.

This book therefore is an attempt to discuss and illustrate how the statistics and metrics that libraries collect and collate, or indeed those that they don't yet collect and collate, can contribute to performance measurement. Whilst the confusion as to what a KPI really is (i.e. at the 2013 statistics workshop) was the initial inspiration behind starting to write this book, I have relaxed a bit, since then with regard to how the terminology of performance indicators and KPIs is used, but one of the objectives of the book is still to illustrate how true KPIs can be used strategically in library and information services and how they form some of the integral tools in our overall performance measurement toolkit.

CHAPTER TWO

What Do KPIs Have to Do With Libraries?

Libraries are at the heart of social systems; they exist to serve the needs of people, to help them live, learn and develop and to act as part of the social glue which holds communities together.

(Brophy, 2006, p. 3)

This book aims to explore performance measurement in libraries, with a particular focus on performance indicators and their role in the performance measurement and quality assurance activity undertaken by many library and information services. Before any such detailed discussion however, it is essential to understand exactly what is meant by 'libraries' and 'information services': what they are, who they are for, what they stand for. Understanding the fundamental nature of libraries can then lead to more effective evaluation, assessment, and performance measurement.

The introductory quote given previously places the library at the heart of society, effectively making it an institution for the people. Feather and Sturges (1997, p. 254) regard a library as 'a collection of materials organised for use', whilst Campbell (2013), writing on the subject of library design suggests that libraries are both 'a collection of books and the space that houses them'.

Unsurprisingly there are several definitions and explanations of the word 'library', most of which depict a physical space with shelves, containing books and other reading materials, but this picture in itself is limited in that the library as a place of reading is not a complete definition as it omits the various other activities which take place within a library, as well as the roles played by a library in human life and society in general (Chowhdury, Burton, McMenemy, & Pulter, 2008).

Similarly these more traditional definitions of 'library' do not appear to take into account the developments of the digital library and information environment and the concept of the 'library without walls'. Perhaps a more accurate understanding of 'libraries' and the context within which they need to be assessed and evaluated can only come about when addressing the contemporary issues as well as the traditional roles and functions of the library.

Libraries and Key Performance Indicators
http://dx.doi.org/10.1016/B978-0-08-100227-8.00002-9

Another factor to consider when trying to understand what a library is, is the profession behind the phenomenon, that of librarianship and the human resource behind the library which makes it function as it is intended. As a profession, librarianship has a core set of values about providing equity of access to information. These are illustrated in Ranganathan's Five Laws of Library Science

1. Books are for use
2. For every reader, his or her book
3. For every book, its reader
4. Save time on the reader
5. A library is a growing organism

(Ranganathan, 1931)

Whilst these values (laws) are now over 80 years old and rather focused on the provision of books, they still stand today as the fundamental values on which libraries and librarianship are founded, and can be interpreted in a more modern and meaningful way:

- Knowledge and information is produced and made available for everyone to use.
- Regardless of demographics or socio-economic status the library will make its knowledge and information resources available to all (or at least all its members/community).
- The library's role is to organise knowledge and information so that it is easily and speedily retrieved and located.
- Library collections are dynamic and are managed accordingly.

In his book *The Library in the Twenty-First Century*, Brophy (2001) goes into much detail about what constitutes a library and takes into account historic and traditional functions and the emerging technological developments which have had a huge impact on librarianship in the 20th century and anticipates the continual changing nature and role of libraries moving into the 21st century. Brophy argues that 'libraries provide a very wide variety of activities and services for people in all walks of life' and that the key concepts of this activity are 'education, information storage and retrieval, and the transmission of knowledge' (Brophy, 2001, p. 14).

Totterdell (2005) discusses the contemporary role of the library in society and suggests that over recent years the focus on the role of libraries in the United Kingdom has changed emphasis within changing political climates. She suggests that the traditional public library in the United Kingdom has been based on four keystones: culture, education, leisure and recreation, and information, and that different political viewpoints have placed various emphases on these four keystones.

Perhaps one of the simplest explanations of the contemporary role of libraries is that librarianship essentially consists of three facets: content, service, and users (Chowdhury et al, 2008, p. 8). These basic facets can be expanded into a number of roles and activities and can encompass all the traditional as well as the emerging roles of libraries and information services.

Narrowing libraries down to these three core fundamental facets makes it easier to understand the nature of libraries and their many roles and functions which in turn are achieved through a variety of processes, methods, and operations including:

- Collection management and development
- Document supply activities such as interlending and digitisation initiatives
- Development of physical study and reading spaces
- Development and maintenance of storage spaces and systems
- Organisation of information through catalogues and indexes
- Provision of electronic resources
- Provision of IT and computing facilities
- Development and delivery of support platforms through teaching, training, and enquiry services
- Preservation and curation of materials

The list could go on, but in effect, a wide variety of work and activity is required in order for libraries to perform their basic function, that of making information available to individuals and the communities which they serve. This can be the public library serving the citizenry and community; an academic library and the services it provides for its students, researchers, and scholars; a health library delivering resources and facilities on its medical, clinical, and nursing specialists; or a specialist library with a unique and focused customer base.

They are ultimately all fulfilling the same role that of providing content (information and knowledge) to its users through a series of services, facilities, resources, and support.

2.1 INFORMATION AND SOCIETY

Information as a commodity is used purposefully by millions of people, all over the world every day. Research, scholarship, knowledge, data, and information are generated and circulated in many ways including through knowledge quarters, publishing and the research activities, and outputs from universities and research institutions. As identified before, one of the roles of the library is to make these information resources available to their user communities. This particular role takes on greater significance when it is within the context of the *Information Society*, which needs to be acknowledged because the shear wealth of content and information available to users in the modern digital library age impacts upon how libraries achieve content delivery to their users.

Mattelart (2003) presents a thorough introduction to the concept of *information society* and provides us with an easy-to-understand overview of the gradual rise of the notion of the *information society*:

A new ideology that dare not speak its name has become part and parcel of 'the nature of things' and suddenly ranks as the dominant paradigm for social change
(Mattelart, 2003, p. 2)

There are not many areas of social, political, and economic activity which have not been affected by the development of information and communication technology, and Mattelart addresses how the information society has conceptualised as a theoretical concept, as well as a global policymaking tool, impacting upon people on a vast and continuous scale.

One of the fundamental issues at the heart of information society is the sheer speed with which new knowledge and information is produced and the impact that this has on its dissemination, let alone critical consumption and ultimate impact and value of knowledge and information. A normative theory of the information society attempts to bring together and address the issues surrounding information in its broadest context in the 21st century, and considers the ever increasing production, distribution, and consumption of information (Duff, 2013). In his discussions about the changing and increasing nature of information Duff talks about the blurring of boundaries and borders:

Shifting, elastic, fuzzy borders have indeed developed between the private and the public, as well as between other social categories, such as commodity and resource, news and entertainment, the nation and the world system.
(Duff, 2013, p. 11)

There can be no doubt that the production of knowledge and information is perpetual and ever increasing. John Feather's work on the information society is very comprehensive and clearly explains the use of information within a variety of economic and cultural environments and also discusses in detail how the commercial value of information becomes increasingly important in a world in which data can be transmitted across the globe in a matter of seconds (Feather, 2013). This in itself suggests a certain pressure on individuals, communities, and organisations to be able to adequately seek, absorb, critique, discern, process, and effectively use information and knowledge, which is of course where libraries play a very significant role.

Studies about the information society also suggest that information production is not shrinking and the difference between types of information is becoming less and less clear. This all leads to the potential for individuals to be overwhelmed by information which can result in potentially disengaging from making use of knowledge and information. This presents a further consideration for libraries in fulfilling their information searching and content provision objectives as well as the roles they play in educating their users in effective information handling.

There is also an emerging 'information obesity' notion, which considers the relationship that individuals have with information in today's information society (Whitworth, 2009). The information society is a complex concept in which equality of access to information is fundamental. Whitworth argues that information obesity occurs: through a lack of understanding of technological change and its consequences, within individuals, communities, and education systems; insufficient opportunity to reflect upon information before absorbing it; economic pressures on citizens to consume information, due to the profits it makes for the information industries; lack of management of the informational environment; lack of creativity within many organisation roles.

Whitworth argues that information obesity has resulted from a failure to use information resources in ways that build within individuals and communities, sustainable foundations for future activity. That is to say that information is not being used to create knowledge and is therefore not embedded by individuals or communities within their own environments. Whitworth approaches his discussions from an educational perspective, with educational strategy being at the heart of the solution to the information obesity problem and other issues resulting from the information society. He talks about the information society being responsible for the emergence of new literacies and questions how individuals and communities are to develop such skills (e.g. digital literacy and information literacy). Libraries and information services have a crucial role to play in the education of their users and in alleviating the sense of overwhelming which can occur through information overload within an information society environment.

Added to this overwhelming amount of information available, there is also nowadays growing pressure, all over the world for all publically funded information and research to be made freely available to the public and for academic institutions in particular to make their research accessible (European Commission, 2013; Finch Group, 2012).

2.2 WHERE DOES EVALUATION FIT IN?

In all instances and across every sector (academic, public, school, prison, health, commercial, etc.) the library enables access to resources and facilities and does this through providing services to its users and customers.

To the users of libraries, the information that they seek, acquire, and use through engaging with their respective library service and the actual services that they receive have a particular and significant value. The value of the resources, facilities, and services to the individual will differ, depending on what their initial requirement was. It might be of monetary value, strategic value, or sentimental, but the information and the library service itself will nevertheless have a value to the individual.

Beyond the value of information gained through interaction with a library, usage of the library itself should also have an impact on the individual user. Where there is impact there should be a measurable or significant change to the circumstance of the individual.

Once we start talking about the value and the impact of the library we are effectively moving into library evaluation and assessment territory and how libraries measure their performance. That is to say how do libraries measure how well they fulfil their roles and responsibilities as defined before?

There are several different ideas about what library evaluation and performance measurement really is and why it should be done. Crawford (2000, p. 10) suggests that the two main reasons are to convince funders and clients that the service is delivering the benefits that were expected when the investment was made; as an internal control mechanism to ensure that the resources are used efficiently and effectively.

These two main reasons can be further segmented into objectives of decision making, quality assurance, problem solving, planning, service improvement, etc. but at the heart of the reasoning is still whether the library is achieving its fundamental objectives of delivering content and information to its users through its services, facilities, and resources.

To this end, libraries have always attempted to measure their performance in order to justify themselves and make business cases for resources and developments. Similarly there is a lot of discussion and debate about how libraries demonstrate and measure their value and impact. Such measurements tend to focus on usage of libraries and resources and metrics around quantities (e.g. number of visits, number of loans, number of downloads). Being able to generate quantitative data about library usage also helps libraries to ascertain how they are being used, how busy they are, and how usage compares statistically with years gone by. Such statistics also allow for libraries to compare their usage with other libraries and derive specific statistics in order to do this (e.g. SCONUL statistics).

The study of library evaluation, assessment, and performance measurement relies on many qualitative methods, which will be discussed in the next chapters. However, being able to use statistical evidence to truly measure performance is becoming increasingly important to libraries as they are required to be more and more accountable to the institutions and communities that they serve. This book will attempt to look at how libraries can use their statistics, data, and management information in order to demonstrate and measure performance. Such information can be used as an indicator as to how a service is performing, although this needs to be within the context of preagreed standards or targets. As such management information can be used as a key performance indicator and ultimately a measurement of business performance.

This book will explore how different types of libraries make use of performance indicators as a performance measurement tool and will place it within a broader library evaluation context.

CHAPTER THREE

A Brief History of Evaluation and Performance Measurement in Libraries

If you are reading this book, you are no doubt interested in library performance measurement and may well be aware of the wealth of literature and discussion available on the reasons why and how library evaluation and performance measurement is carried out. This chapter will attempt to address the 'why' part of this discussion and in doing so presents a concise background to library assessment and evaluation and in particular why libraries engage in performance measurement activity.

> Performance measurement is central to library management, since without a firm grasp on what is actually being achieved it is impossible to move forward to improved service, or even to maintain the status quo
>
> **(Brophy, 2006, p. 1)**

This stance suggests that without evaluation and performance measurement a library simply cannot deliver its mission, either in the present or in the future. Librarians and information professionals have measured the quality, the performance, and the impact of their services for a long time in order to inform just this: how they operate in the present and how they might operate in the future. It could be argued that the present measure of performance, and the judgement made on how well the library is performing provides the benchmark as to how the library should be performing in the future. That is to say, performance measurement and evaluation are used in order to make comparative assessments against standards and targets, and to make judgements against this performance in order to set targets for future performance. Part of this judgement and target setting (or anticipating outcomes) is to evaluate and analyse the effects that the library service has on its users.

3.1 WHAT IS BEING MEASURED?

The value and impact that a library service has on its users and the capability a library has in meeting its user needs become key criteria for

Libraries and Key Performance Indicators
http://dx.doi.org/10.1016/B978-0-08-100227-8.00003-0

assessing the quality of that service. Orr (1973) writes that "the value of a service must ultimately be judged in terms of the beneficial effects accruing from its use." This notion of evaluating a library's value and benefits it has on the user at first appears simple and easy to justify why a library might engage in evaluation in order to demonstrate these attributes. However, the benefits realised by a library, or indeed any surface, lead to discussion as to how the service has had an impact on an individual or a group, and in turn about measuring the performance of the service. Therefore on closer inspection and investigation it becomes clear that there are several interpretations of both value and impact and a subsequent wealth of potential methods as to how one might go about their measurement. This is what makes the study of library evaluation, assessment, and performance measurement so fascinating.

John Crawford (2006) writes about the evolving culture of evaluation in library and information services and in doing so debates and discusses the various mindsets, attitudes, and cultures within the librarianship profession and attempts to make sense of why as a profession there are a variety of methodologies, approaches, toolkits, and instruments used for evaluation as well as a diversity of drivers and rationales for conducting detailed evaluation into service provision. He contextualises the requirements for demonstrating value and impact across the public sector and in the public services and establishes various trends and differences across the sectors which contribute to this. From these and other discussions it is possible to piece together a brief chronology of key moments in library evaluation history which lead us to the complexities of today.

3.2 KEY MOMENTS IN LIBRARY EVALUATION HISTORY—HOW IT ALL BEGAN

Is library evaluation and performance measurement something new? Much of the discussion suggests that the culture became dominant and prominent during the 1970s due to the growth of consumerism. During this period consumers were encouraged to view the quality of goods and services that they received much more critically and to complain if they were not satisfied. It is also during this period, from 1976 onwards, that the United Kingdom saw declining patterns of public expenditure which signalled the need to maximise resources and defend preexisting patterns of expenditure (Crawford, 2000). This of course required data about library usage and impact and therefore could be regarded as a pivotal moment in the history of library performance.

However, the consumer movement of the 1970s cannot be held singularly responsible for the development of a 'customer facing' culture in libraries. Crawford (2006) uses three great historical examples of library evaluation within this context. First, he acknowledges the 1931 report from the University of Oxford's Bodleian Library, which reports back on the findings of an extensive study into the resources, services, and facilities provided by the library to its scholars. The report was informed through data collected from a whole range of stakeholders (Crawford, 2006, p. 2). Crawford's second modern historical example is that of the Edinburgh Public Libraries Survey of 1936. This survey was regarded as quite radical in that an analysis of all the books on loan (and to whom) on a particular date was undertaken, and this subsequently determined the further developments and investments into Edinburgh's city centre-based central library and its suburban branch libraries (Crawford, 2006, p. 5). Crawford's third historical reference is to *The Londoner and His Library* (Groombridge, 1964) which followed a mass observation survey undertaken in 1947. This study analysed and critiqued the seemingly inadequate services and facilities offered by public library services and concluded that whilst public libraries were held in high regard, most people did not belong to them on account of their inaccessibility and underperformance. The report is thought to include the first mentions of *satisfaction* with library services and discusses *value* and *impact* and talks about *social inclusion* (Crawford, 2006).

However, it can be argued that the well known mathematician and librarian, Samuel Clement Bradford first brought about the notion of library performance measurement in the 1948 work *Documentation*, in which *Bradford's law* (the law of scattering) is developed, regarding the difference in demand for scientific journals (Bradford, 1948). This work in turn is said to have influenced further work on bibliometrics and citation analysis of scientific publications, and as such can be regarded as a keystone in library evaluation literature.

Philip Morse (1968) was the first to dedicate an entire tome to the theme of library evaluation and his book *Library Effectiveness* is widely regarded as ground breaking in this respect (Brophy, 2006, p. 1) Morse's work establishes some of the key topics, themes, objectives, and practices of library evaluation, which takes on a greater significance a decade later, when library performance measurement becomes a key managerial operation in the new consumer society.

3.3 THE CONSUMER SOCIETY

Crawford (2006, p. 6) suggests that in the 1960s Aslib noted that the purpose of libraries was to satisfy their readers, but observed that very little had been done to find out how satisfied readers really were, and it is the growth of the aforementioned consumer movement in the 1970s which encouraged the users of goods and services to view them much more critically and question the quality that they were receiving. This consumer society then led to a more sophisticated approach to measuring satisfaction with service and overall performance management of libraries. It is during this period that the concept of *effectiveness* and *value* of service became more important and libraries began to be judged and assessed against how well they met their intended objectives (Blagden & Harrington, 1990). The idea of library usage as an indicator of effectiveness and value also emerged and annual monitoring of performance became an annual activity for many libraries.

Since this time, performance measurement of libraries has been regarded as a key management and administration function, required in order to justify library services, make cases for development, and continually improve libraries in response to customer expectations. There are a therefore a lot of practical texts available to assist library managers to perform these functions. One early and significant work on measuring and evaluating library services, by Lancaster and Jonich, suggests that, put simply "evaluation consists of the comparison of the performance with the objectives of the agency, in order to determine (a) whether there has been any change in performance for a given time period, (b) if so, whether the change is in the desired direction, and (c) if so, to what extent." (Lancaster & Jonich, 1977, vii).

3.4 NEW MANAGERIALISM

Consumerism gave rise to a much more customer-oriented service culture in the United Kingdom by the1990s. Having emerged from the retail sector, it was not long until this movement transferred into the public services. Performance frameworks such as The Citizens' Charter and The Audit Commission's Best Value Inspectorate have influenced a regime of evaluation for libraries (Crawford, 2000, p. 3) whilst quality initiatives such as British and International standards for libraries (BS/EN/ISO9000) and the Cabinet Office's Customer Service Excellence Award (Formerly Charter

Mark) have allowed libraries, across all sectors to aim for excellence and achieve accreditation for achieving this. This modern culture of assessment and evaluation is cross sectoral and the 1990s are regarded as being responsible for a 'new managerialism' in libraries, which puts an emphasis on strategic planning and customer service and on libraries having mission statements and core objectives which can be used as a baseline for evaluation (Crawford, 2006, p. 11).

As a result more sophisticated methods, techniques, and frameworks were developed so that libraries could really focus on using library data and metrics in order to demonstrate 'time and motion' studies and 'cost effectiveness' of services (Lancaster, 1993). Lancaster provides examples and formula which can be used to demonstrate performance through figures and metrics and in doing so provides a framework for developing library performance indicators as a means of evaluation. He also suggests that in order to fully demonstrate quality a library must collect data which reflect upon the 'success' of the service. This period of new managerialism introduces a mixed method approach to library evaluation where metrics and statistical indicators (e.g. library usage, survey data, and analysis) need to be complemented with perhaps deeper qualitative data (e.g. suggestion schemes, focus groups) in order to fully inform evaluation and make performance-related decisions.

3.5 DEMONSTRATING QUALITY

In order to be accountable to stakeholders, customers, and funding bodies, libraries have to be able to demonstrate the quality of what they offer which brought with it the management paradigm of quality management. There is much written about quality management and indeed quality management in the library and information profession. With this being the case there are several suggestions as to what quality looks like including quality as exceptional or something special, quality as perfection, quality as fitness for purpose, quality as value for money, quality as change and transformation. Roberts and Rowley (2004), when writing about quality management suggest that in the library and information sector the focus is on service quality and needs to involve processes to measure and improve service quality and similarly measures to set targets and monitor progress against them. Another strategic library management writer, Corral suggests that:

*Quality is an overused and poorly understood word in the vocabulary of manage-
ment. It is a recurring theme in missions, goals and objectives and often seems to
add little of substance to such statements.*

(Corrall, 2000, pp. 219–220)

However, Corrall then goes on to say that while there is no single accepted
definition of quality in the management literature there is agreement about
its meaning within a management context, that of fitness for purpose or
meeting agreed expectations or requirements.

The opening chapter looked at some of the background behind performance measurement and one of the key reasons for employing performance
measurement techniques is to be able to demonstrate the quality achieved by
the library. Therefore defining quality and anticipating what a 'quality service' looks like becomes necessary, and where library and information managers previously looked at justifying their services through measuring usage,
finding measures for 'quality' posed new challenges which is why impact and
value have become established as service outcomes by which quality can be
measured. The shift in focus as to what makes a quality library and information service to be on outcomes, values, and impact is a very significant point
as it places the library user at the centre of the quality debate. The 'new managerialism' which has already been discussed centres around whether the
library user has a positive experience of using the library, whether the outcomes of their library use are beneficial, whether their library use results in a
positive impact, and how much do they value their library and their experiences of using it. To any new professionals reading this, this the notion of a
positive user experience will seem like an obvious place to focus quality processes, but it is in fact only recently that library and information services have
placed the customer and the community ahead of their collections, and
placed access to information over ownership of resources. That is to say that
it is still not too long ago when the library's main concern was the richness
and depth of its collection. Indeed Carr (2006) recalls the era as a time when
"users where seen as an irritant and were expected to be grateful for what
librarians decided they needed." Whilst Carr was speaking about academic
libraries, this could have been said for the entire library and information sector and it is the increasing availability of online information and its accessibility which has forced the library and information sector to think carefully
about how services are provided and managed and in turn to consider the
needs, demands, and expectations of the library user at the heart of this.

Chapters 6–8 will look at some of the different methods currently used to
measure the quality and performance of a library service and will consider

both quantitative and qualitative methods, but the theme of 'quality for the user' will be recurring.

Crawford (2006, p. 22) suggests that in order to get a complete picture of the quality of library services a combination of measures and techniques are necessary including charters and codes of practice, service standards, performance indicators and statistics, surveys and qualitative methods, unobtrusive testing such as mystery shopping, commitment and involvement of all levels of staff, third part accreditation and awards.

This is in fact a very neat list of all the potential facets and stages of a quality assurance framework. Developing customer charters and service standards are an excellent way of defining quality and effectively setting standards of quality which the library needs to achieve and demonstrate. This in turn helps to manage customer expectation and makes defining and measuring the quality of a service achievable. Similarly, involving library staff and engaging with stakeholders in defining quality and ensuring that library services and facilities are developed and improved upon in response to their quality measures form an integral part of the quality cycle.

CHAPTER FOUR

Developing a Culture of Performance Measurement

You might ask 'why do we need a culture of performance measurement in libraries?' The simple answer to this question is because libraries need to demonstrate that they are of use, that they are valuable and that they are valued, that they are good and for good. This then leads to the question '*what makes a good library?*' and how do researchers, practitioners, and stakeholders view '*goodness*' in a library context. A key study here is Orr's '*Measuring the Goodness of Library Services*' in which he suggests that libraries need to frame evaluation against two key questions: 'How good is this library?' and 'How much good does this library do?'

For the majority of library users and stakeholders there is an acceptance that libraries are indeed 'good'. They are the houses of knowledge, scholarship, and learning and librarians act as wise, supportive, and professional gatekeepers to this knowledge. Collectively, the space, the resources, and the support lead 'good' things: developments and improvements in society and organisations, advances in research and scholarship, a well informed and better educated citizenry and a general.

The flaw in this sweeping statement is that it is in fact just that, a sweeping statement. Subconscious feelings and general acceptances are not particularly scientific ways in which to measure or demonstrate the 'goodness' of a library, although many commentators and library users would be satisfied in knowing that the 'goodness' of a library cannot effectively be measured and would suggest that we should just agree that libraries are indeed 'good'.

In the case of academic libraries, according to Munde and Marks, there was a long held view that they provide a fundamental societal 'good' which fostered a belief that that there was no need to justify or defend them. This culture was then reflected in the widely held belief that librarians were the gatekeepers to knowledge and that they knew what was best for their patrons. There was no need to consult with patrons or collect data because librarians could make decisions based upon their experience, anecdotal reports, or their feelings (Munde & Marks, 2009, p. 19).

Libraries and Key Performance Indicators
http://dx.doi.org/10.1016/B978-0-08-100227-8.00004-2

It would appear that without intervention there may have been a danger of a culture of 'nonevaluation' emerging with librarians relying on instinct and acceptance as performance measurement techniques. This was never going to happen, once 'patrons' became consumers and libraries as resource-intensive services became more and more accountable to the communities and organisations which provided those resources. The notion of demonstrating 'goodness' quickly turned into that of demonstrating 'quality', which then leads to the more familiar contemporary questions which we would ask about effectiveness, efficiency, economic value, and impact.

This effectively means that performance measurement becomes a strand of quality management, and the challenge for librarians is how to reconcile their very broad and potentially conflicting views of quality. Evaluation and performance measurement allow for some sort of objectivity and allow for librarians to investigate and define the characteristics which make up the quality of their service. Quality is relative and is linked to the expectations of the library's users. Being informed about those expectations and setting objective measures to test how well the library is meeting those expectations, and a willingness to change and improve if found to be faltering, is essentially why libraries need to adopt a culture of assessment and evaluation. Performance measurement becomes a modern and more scientific way of demonstrating the 'goodness' of the library.

4.1 WHAT IS ACTUALLY BEING EVALUATED?

The simple answer to this question is 'everything about the library needs to be evaluated', but as with everything else connected to library evaluation it is not quite that simple. Munde and Marks make the point that within the library assessment culture there is a danger that library data is gathered but has no relevance to the decision-making process or is gathered and simply not used (Munde & Marks, 2009, p. 6).

Crawford (2006) suggests that to get a complete picture of quality of library services a combination of methods of evaluation and measures needs to be in place including customer charters and standards, performance indicators, surveys and qualitative methods, and third party audits and investigations.

These methods along with how raw statistical and qualitative data is used within library evaluation will be discussed in the next chapters, but one area which almost underpins performance measurement is that of value and impact. How users value libraries and the impact that libraries have on their users are largely intangible concepts, yet one of the main objectives of library evaluation is to demonstrate success in these areas. How libraries achieve this through both quantitative and qualitative methods becomes very complex and has indeed been part of a much wider discussion.

4.2 DEMONSTRATING IMPACT

I didn't cry when I was homeless. The tears came later. I needed to care for my son and the library provided me an enchanted world to share with him. We arrived every day as the doors opened. My eager boy discovered dinosaurs, befriended librarians, and developed an on-going love of books. I devoured stories of others who face challenges. We shared story time and played on the lawn. Though homeless, the library helped me to mother my son by allowing me to give when I had nothing to spend.

Dowd (1996, p. 162)

This quotation from Dowd's study of homelessness and public libraries in 1996 provides a great example of how library impact can be demonstrated and documented. Libraries, across all sectors serve a particular purpose and set out to achieve goals and objectives as determined by the library's stakeholders. Such objectives will differ according to the nature and strategic function of the library and what the particular expectations of its user community are. If the library delivers its objectives effectively and achieves its aims or goals then there is a high likelihood that the library will have had an impact on the users and the communities which it serves, and through having an impact will be considered valuable, or to have value (either financial or otherwise) by those who use the library's services and facilities. The library which is the subject of the previous quotation clearly had an impact upon and a value for the individual mother and son in the example and this is evidenced in the testimonial. However, outside of anecdotes such as this, capturing such evidence of value and impact of libraries and developing frameworks by which to measure them does not appear to be common place and is certainly not standardised where measurement activity is practised. In effect, it is nearly impossible to separate library impact from other influences and to prove that changes in circumstances, situations, competences, or behaviours are indeed an effect of using library services (Poll & Payne, 2006, p. 3).

4.3 OUTCOMES OF LIBRARY USAGE

Not being able to discern library impact from other potential influences is one of the main frustrations of the library assessor. That is, unless, the assessor is fully aware of what the library was trying to achieve in the first instance. This is where the concept of 'outcome' becomes important in the world of library evaluation and performance measurement. Before library impact and value can truly be evaluated, or before performance can be measured, the intended outcome of the library and benefits to the customer need to be explicit. Performance outcomes form part of the strategic management and planning of the library and need to be closely linked to the library's mission and core aims.

Understanding the answers to the question 'what is the library trying to achieve?' is fundamental if the library is going to be able to demonstrate how it makes a difference to the customer. Understanding the library customer, their demands and expectations, and their loyalty is key to being able to identifying success criteria and impact indicators (Hernon & Altman, 2010). Setting indicators against intended outcomes is one way of addressing this. Designing such indicators is one of the most crucial steps in the whole process of evaluating impact. This is one of the more difficult parts of library evaluation to get right as there is a tendency for library managers to design indicators that are easy to measure (i.e. around usage) rather than around outcome (Markless & Streatfield, 2006).

In discussing 'library outcomes' there is a general acceptance that libraries need to demonstrate beneficial 'outcomes' to their users. Good examples of such outcomes could be around: knowledge gained by users; higher information literacy competencies; higher academic or professional success; social inclusion; or, an increase in individual well-being (Poll & Payne, 2006).

However, there is no internationally agreed or tested method for assessing the different aspects of library 'outcomes'. Indeed the recognised International Standard on performance indicators in libraries is quite clear when it states that "it does not include performance indicators for the evaluation of the outcomes of library services either on individuals, the communities that libraries serve, or on society…" (British Standards Institute, 2008, v)

This is not to say that library assessors should just give up on trying to evaluate impact against outcomes, but that the British Standards Institute do not recommend any particular performance indicators for doing this.

A larger scale example in the UK higher education community is that of the *LIRG/SCONUL Impact Initiative*, which looked to assess the impact of higher education libraries on specific outcomes around learning, teaching, and research in UK universities (Markless & Streatfield, 2005). The initiative then sought to develop methodologies to be used by libraries to measure their impact against these outcomes including:

- Deeper understanding of how libraries support academic processes
- Improved dialogue with academics and stakeholders
- Library staff development
- Raised profile for the library

As part of the wider project Markless and Streatfield (2006) report how, as a result of using their new impact assessment methodology, they were able to make positive changes in the way they approach information skills and information literacy training with both academic staff and students at their institution. Put briefly, the intended outcome of the project was an improved and more effective information skills programme, which was achieved and had a beneficial impact. The assessment methodology allowed them to measure this to ensure that they were on course for achieving the desired outcome.

On a broader scale the overall results of the *LIRG/SCONUL Impact Initiative* included an enabling and greater understanding of outcomes-based performance measurement in academic libraries. The project effectively achieves this, as well as developing a useful toolkit and set of case studies for the academic library community.

Huysmans and Oomes (2013) conducted a literature review, on a global scale, about the societal impact that public libraries have on their communities. The findings of this literature review, identify, and conceptually enrich five particular areas of impact: cognitive, social, cultural, affective, and economic. These are good examples of broad, general outcomes against which libraries are able to measure their performance and impact.

Having established that performance outcomes are an important building block with regard to measuring impact, it is possible for libraries to set quite specific performance outcomes and objectives. Good examples of these can be found in the health libraries sector. Value and impact studies are commonplace in this sector and their longitudinal application can be attributed to the development of evidence-based practice within health and clinical settings. One particular piece of recent research in this area demonstrates that clinical librarians have a variety of positive impacts of the information-seeking behaviour of clinicians and health care professionals with whom they worked, and therefore ultimately on patient care and well-being (Marshall, 2007).

4.4 SOCIAL IMPACT

Outcomes of library activity or strategy can be very specific (i.e. in the case of the *LIRG/SCONUL Impact Initiative*) or indeed very broad or general. These could be regarded as the two extremes of the library performance 'measurability' scale. An example of a broad outcome would be that of changes to behaviours of culture, which by their very nature are more difficult to measure than very specific outcomes. Subsequently, libraries that wish to demonstrate outcomes relating to social impact or economic impact often find it difficult to do so.

Social impact is most frequently associated with public library services and the impact that they have on their communities and constituents (Kerslake & Kinnel, 1997).

The services offered by the public library are diverse and their target audience is equally so. This is a major difference between the public library sector and other sectors (academic, school, specialist, health). Whilst the other sectors still have a diversity of users they could certainly be regarded as more homogenous that that of any public library, whose users comprise all individuals and citizens within their communities, spanning demographic, age, and class boundaries such as children, ethnic minorities, disabled, homeless, etc. Having such a variety of users and user groups allows for a richness of services and a deeper and potentially more varied impact on a larger number of users, but also further complicates how that impact is measured, and certainly if it is to be measured in a standard format.

Social impact is clearly something that public libraries have taken very seriously and have used several different methods to try to measure and demonstrate this.

Using a 'social audit' approach, Linley and Usherwood (1998) try to enable a 'sensible measurement' of the public sector outcomes that UK libraries needed to demonstrate in the 1990s. This is achieved to some extent, but in effect the study simply reiterates the perceived value that public libraries have in all aspects of community life. The two case studies used in the study (Newcastle and Somerset Library Authorities) provide a lot of anecdotal evidence of the perceived value, worth, and impact of their respective public library services. The case studies, though quite different in nature and approach generate a lot of valuable discussion about the complexity of public library services and the impact they clearly have on community and citizenship.

McMenemy (2009) takes a very comprehensive look at measuring public library performance in the United Kingdom and suggests that in England in particular, the focus of public library performance measurement has changed from a best value regime (using standardised Annual Library Plans) in the 1990s to that of comprehensive area assessments within council-run public services in 2009. Comprehensive area assessments focus on people and places, providing a snapshot of life in a local area on an annual basis and are designed to help people understand if they are getting value for money from their local services (Audit Commission, 2009).

4.5 VALUE

A typical dictionary definition might suggest that evaluation is the 'assessment of value' of an activity or object. The financial value of libraries is often questioned and impact is assessed with this in mind. The results of such assessment effectively go into justifying the value of the library with regards to the justification of resources, improvement of services, etc.

A recent development in assessing the impact of public libraries in the United Kingdom has seen a movement to ascertain the economic value that they provide. McMenemy (2009) discusses how measuring outputs alongside the measurement of economic impacts should provide evidence of value for money, but also introduces the system of contingent valuation, which aims to survey users as well as nonusers in assessing a public library's economic value. He draws upon the work of Aabo and Audunsen (2002) who discuss in greater detail the rational choice theory behind contingent evaluation in that individuals must anticipate the outcomes of alternative course of action and calculate that which will be best for them.

Contingent valuation involves constructing a market by interviewing potential users of that market (or service). It uses a mechanism for eliciting value from the respondent and takes into account the respondent's socioeconomic characteristics, attitudes, and behaviours towards the service (or commodity). Contingent valuation is key to understanding how measuring the value and impact of a public service can really work, as it can be used for measuring the values that nonusers place on a library service, something that more traditional quantitative and qualitative measures cannot do. For example, a person who does not use the public library will have no opinion on the quality of its collections, but they may still place value on the public library's collections in terms of its worth to society (McMenemy, 2009, p. 156). This method has been used to demonstrate return on investment for every pound/dollar spent on a public library service. An example of where this method has been applied to demonstrate return on investment is the British Library, when findings suggested that for every £1.00 spent on the service, a return of £4.00 was generated in terms of public good, knowledge transfer, intellectual capital, etc. (Pung, Clarke, & Patten, 2004).

However, assessing the value of libraries exclusively in economic terms can be a dangerous practice, particularly while public libraries in the United Kingdom are increasingly being asked to justify their contributions to society. If a public library is seen to add less economic value than that which is spent on it, this will potentially negate the wider value and impact that it has on its community.

Value is often linked to statistical evidence, particularly when it comes to gaining value from tangible assets. Therefore the culture of library evaluation can often focus on figures and usage statistics (e.g. amount spent on books, number of active users, number of loans, number of loans per user, amount spent per user, etc.). Indeed, such statistical data about the quantity of usage can show, to some extent, how much a library's services and resources have been drawn upon and there is a perception that high usage indicates that the service is beneficial to its users. However, usage is not synonymous with value. Denise Troll (2001) argues very convincingly that as libraries had been developing their collections and resources very responsively in preparation for the digital age that we now live in, they had, in general, failed to develop strategies and frameworks for measuring library usage in such a way that impact could be demonstrated. She suggests that libraries are still trying to demonstrate impact and value through usage figures, whether it be a decline in gate counts and interlibrary loan requests to large increases in e-resource usage, whereas in actual fact this is simply demonstrating usage of a library which reflects the changing nature of the information and knowledge resources being made available to library users, and not the changing nature of the librarian's professional skills required to deliver services in the digital age.

Whilst practicing librarians may want to use their statistical data about their tangible assets as value measures, there is also some discussion around the value of a library service's intangible assets, such as the human resources involved in running a library service. Being able to demonstrate the impact of the professional librarian on the library user's experience is paramount.

Stephen Town (2011) argues that performance measurement techniques which focus on library output, activity-based costing, and management information are insufficient and suggest that libraries require an 'indication of transcendent contribution that is beyond the immediate or currently recognised temporal, spatial, and influential boundaries of libraries' (Town, 2011, p. 111).

The 'values scorecard' is a tool often referred to when attempting to demonstrate library value. Such a 'scorecard' approach uses four dimensions with which library value can be measured: Relational capital (reputation and reach of the library); Library capital (tangible assets such as collections and services and intangible assets such as meta assets, organisational capital, and human capital); Library virtue (the library's contribution to other agendas such as employability, widening access, etc.); and Library momentum. It is suggested that the most significant aspect of these dimensions, as far as adding value is concerned, is that of human capital (Town & Kyrillidon, 2012). Town also argues that most substantial academic and research libraries invest around half their revenue budgets in staffing and whilst a great deal of effort is expended on the management of this asset, this is not usually accompanied by a similar degree of measurement and evaluation from a value perspective (Town, 2011).

External standards and achievement of kite mark status is a further way of demonstrating added value to library users. The externally awarded 'Charter Mark' and its successor the 'Customer Service Excellence' award operates on three levels: as a driver for continuous improvement, as a tool for skills development, and to demonstrate competence via accreditations to the standard (UK Government Cabinet Office, 2010). Customer Service Excellence, and other similar kite marks, are about exactly this and are excellent instruments and frameworks which a library can use to set service standards and measure themselves against them. As recognition of a library's performance, these external standards do indeed get a 'value message' across to the library's customers (Broady-Preston & Lobo, 2011).

The highly acclaimed 'Lib-Value' project, conducted in the United States, segments its research projects very widely and includes projects aimed at identifying the value of e-books, the use and impact of learning commons spaces, environmental impact of libraries, the impact of information skills teaching, and return on investment of academic libraries (Mays, Tenopir, & Kaufman, 2010).

CHAPTER FIVE

Performance Measurement in the Digital Age

A peculiarity within the library evaluation and assessment culture is a desire to treat the performance measurement and evaluation of the electronic or digital library as something separate to the physical library service. Perhaps it is because library technology and systems such as databases and resource discovery solutions automatically generate usage statistics and analytics that librarians feel they have to treat them differently. Crawford (2006) suggests that evaluating traditional and networked services together leads to confused data and results, and potentially erroneous conclusions regarding perceptions of outcomes and quality of service. Franklin and Plum (2008) suggest that "until the emergence of the digital library environment, evaluating the value and impact of the use of (print) library resources would have at the least been problematic." Their now outdated observations present a neat and concise overview of how this might have been addressed in years gone by and suggesting that "librarians typically relied on gross circulation counts and routinely employed unscientific and unreliable sampling plans and primitive in-house data collection methods such as asking users not to re-shelve library materials so that the library could count them" (Franklin & Plum, 2008, p. 42).

Bertot (2004) argues that the differences lie in the fact that when users provide feedback about electronic information resources they are providing feedback about a service which is not actually provided by the library. This stance suggests that the library should not be held responsible for the quality of the information which is searched for and obtained, nor the system by which it is acquired. This is no longer a valid argument, particularly as libraries offer access to more and more digital and outsourced material. It is how the user engages with the system for searching and obtaining information and then how the information itself is supported and used that constitutes the holistic 'library experience'. The library user will include all the attributes which make up the experience when assessing whether the library adds value, makes an impact, or benefits the individual.

Libraries and Key Performance Indicators
http://dx.doi.org/10.1016/B978-0-08-100227-8.00005-4

Anderson argues that the rise of digital libraries and their accessibility has changed the ultimate mission of academic and research libraries, in that subsequently they play more of a role within the institutional repository, institutional publishing, and research data management environments (Anderson, 2010, p. 53). However, it is not exclusively research and academic libraries whose roles, remits, and missions have changed as a result of developments in electronic resources and scholarly communications. These developments change the ways in which all libraries from all sectors acquire, manage, process, and make accessible the information resources they are responsible for.

There is no doubt that the quantitative measurement of usage of electronic library resources is made easier through automated systems and reporting functionality, and similarly it might be easier to derive particular metrics from using multiple statistics, but that is not to say that this immediately means that value and impact against performance outputs can be measured more easily, or indeed any differently. The modern day 'Information Society' has brought with it decades of technological developments and advancements. This includes innumerable library and information-focused systems including library management, catalogue, e-library, resource discovery, and repository systems. The growth in library technology has brought with it a new type of library evaluation, that of the evaluation of the usability and the usefulness of digital libraries and digital library systems (Buchanan & Salako, 2009). For example, Hoeppner (2012) shares lots of tips for evaluating web-scale discovery systems with regard to their functionality, what is available on the market, selection, and implementation. These are all systems, which as well as serving functional purposes to the delivery of library services, can also generate all types of usage data to illustrate to what extent they have been performing their functions. The digital library environment has made usage information and analytics much more accessible. Welker (2012) discusses the 'joy of gathering and analysing usage statistics, important for evaluating the effectiveness of resources and for making important budgeting decisions.'

It is clear from the previous discussions that what is being evaluated in this new digital library environment is in actual fact the systems themselves and the quality of the information that the systems generate access to, rather than the impact and the value that using these systems can have. It may have made access to usage statistics much easier and brought about a new era of 'systems evaluation' but the basic concepts of a library being a system by which information can be accessed, and the usage of that information remains the same.

One of the characteristics of the 'hybrid' library is that it brings together a range of technologies from different sources in the context of a working library and explores integrated systems and services in both electronic and print environments (Brophy, 2001). Usage data, whether collected manually or enabled through automated systems is still only usage, and as has already been established, usage does not necessarily indicate value or impact. However, an example of where automated usage data has been very well used to attempt to demonstrate the impact of using a library is the 'Library Impact Data Project' carried out in 2011–12 across a number of academic libraries. This project looked at the number of visits to the library, number of book loans, and number of e-resource downloads that individual students made to see if there was any correlation with their ultimate degree award (Stone, Pattern, & Ramsden, 2012). The project was carried out using data from a number of university libraries and is regarded as a major initiative in using usage data to demonstrate impact.

Marr (2015a, 2015b) writes extensively about using data and metrics to make better decisions and improve performance. He argues that even though we have more data than ever before and many new forms of data, it is only useful if we can use it make decisions and to make improvements (Marr, 2015a, 2015b, p. 57). He goes on to talk about everything we do, leaving a digital trace and that both structured data (e.g. financial data, customer data) and unstructured data (e.g. photos, graphics, websites, text files, social media, etc.) could and should be used in the new 'Big Data' environment. The emerging discussions about 'Big Data' therefore have an impact on how we measure performance of the electronic and digital library platforms that form a fundamental part of library and information service provision, and also how the plethora of digital data available about all elements of library and information use can holistically be used to measure library performance.

Another simultaneously emerging discussion is that of 'Altmetrics', and how electronic data, statistics, and metrics can be used to demonstrate the impact of scholarly communications. Altmetrics attempts to take the place of journal impact factors and citation counting. In the new digital and scholarly communications age, where the library can act as publisher and repository as well as the gatekeeper to scholarly information this may need to be considered as a new method of library performance measurement (Brown, 2014).

Altmetrics takes into account scholarly communications (and perhaps library) activity and usage through using 'alternative' metrics, such as those made available through social media channels. Altmetrics will surely have an impact on the library performance measurement environment and will be discussed in more detail in a later chapter.

5.1 WHAT NEXT?

Libraries have been rapidly developing their collections and resources very responsively in preparation for the digital age that we now live in, but have been slower to develop strategies and frameworks for measuring library usage in such a way that impact can be demonstrated. Many libraries are still in fact trying to demonstrate impact through usage figures, whether it is a decline in gate counts and interlibrary loan requests to large increases in e-resource usage, whereas in actual fact this is simply demonstrating usage of a library which reflects the changing nature of the information and knowledge resources being made available to library users, and not the changing nature of the librarian's professional skills required to deliver services in the digital age. Being able to demonstrate the impact of the professional librarian on the library user's experience is paramount.

CHAPTER SIX

Quantitative Methods of Performance Measurement

6.1 STATISTICS AND STATISTICAL RETURNS

Library and information professionals like to count things and library and information services are full of things that can be counted: library visits, library users, issues, returns, renewals, fines, enquiries, photocopies, print-outs, desks, chairs, computers, books, journal titles, journal issues, e-journal titles, e-journal searches, e-journal downloads, e-book downloads, interlibrary loans, etc. the list is potentially endless. In addition, it is also often easy to quantify other elements of the management of libraries, namely the number of staff and the amount of financial resource required to run the service.

A lot of time and resource is spent by library administrators counting items and transactions associated with their service delivery and indeed there is a lot of professional interest in doing so. All library sectors are encouraged to count and provide usage statistics to their stakeholders or to compare and benchmark themselves against other library services (or other competing services) and several current examples are provided later.

Ironically, in research terms, quantitative measures and methods are often regarded as more robust and credible than qualitative measures, but whilst there is a lot of interest in statistical returning within the library and information profession, it is quite often dismissed as inadequate when it comes to discussions around measures for demonstrating value and impact. This is because by themselves statistical measures tend not to demonstrate anything other than library usage. These statistics are in fact an excellent measure for demonstrating library usage and are often used to demonstrate how busy a service is or, on the contrary, how it is no longer as busy as it used to be. Usage figures and resource statistics, when compared with other institutions or against previous years in a time series analysis can tell part of the story of a particular library and this in turn can be used for justifying services

Libraries and Key Performance Indicators
http://dx.doi.org/10.1016/B978-0-08-100227-8.00006-6

or making business cases. Similarly derived statistics which can show amount of spend per library user, or number of staff per library user, for example, can be used to present a case to stakeholders. Usage statistics also make useful management information and often service and resource decisions can be made by analysing such data. For example, usage figures of printed and electronic resources can be used to determine the spending on similar resources in the next budget year, or changes to opening hours can be made based on which times or days are statistically the most popular.

6.2 CURRENT EXAMPLES OF LIBRARY STATISTICAL RETURNING

A useful current example of collecting usage statistics is the *SCONUL Statistical Return* mentioned before. The Society of College, National and University Libraries (SCONUL)[1] represents all university libraries in the United Kingdom and Ireland and many of the UK's colleges of higher education. The society promotes awareness of the role of academic libraries and represents their views and interests to government, regulators, and other stakeholders. It helps academic libraries collaborate to deliver services efficiently, including through shared services, and to share knowledge and best practice. This includes survey and evaluation work and the co-ordination of the annual statistical return in which most of SCONUL's 184 members return a comprehensive set of annual usage figures. Once collated and analysed, these usage figures are published as the *Annual Library Statistics* and continue to be well used by libraries to benchmark and compare against other institutions and to present management information about library usage to stakeholders.

Meanwhile in the United States the National Center for Education Statistics (NCES)[2] collects data biennially from approximately 3700-degree awarding university and postsecondary education institutions in order to provide an overview of academic library usage nationwide and by state.

The Association of Research Libraries (ARL)[3] is a consortium of 125 research libraries at research universities and institutions in the United States and Canada, which share similar research-oriented missions and aspirations. ARL plays a similar role to that of SCONUL in the United Kingdom in its

[1] http://www.sconul.ac.uk/.

[2] http://nces.ed.gov/surveys/libraries/academic.asp.

[3] http://www.arl.org/.

development and application of academic library statistics, performance measures, and analytics, both for internal use by the member institutions and for benchmarking and collaboration purposes.

Such consortium approaches to statistical returning clearly benefit the membership with regard to standardising statistics and metrics and enabling comparative analysis and benchmarking. Another such example is the Australian and New Zealand academic library statistics which are collected and published annually for the Council of Australian University Libraries (CAUL),[4] which currently includes statistics for 39 Australian, 8 New Zealand, and 2 co-operative areas.

These organisations which co-ordinate statistical returning amongst higher education libraries have enjoyed a period of sustainability which actually helps with consistency and time series analytic comparisons amongst member institutions. Statistical data collection, along with other collaborative quantitative and qualitative performance measurement initiatives in other sectors has not necessarily enjoyed the same consistency.

Nevertheless, there is still a lot of very good practice to report upon. For example, the Council for Learning and Resources in Colleges (CoLRIC),[5] the professional association for Further Education libraries in the United Kingdom has established an annual survey of Library and Learning Resources Services in FE and sixth form colleges. The survey collects basic usage statistics, but does so in a derived fashion which makes survey results comparable against a set of performance and impact indicators. In this instance the survey provides both quantitative and qualitative data as the indicators focus on the qualitative aspect of learning resources. For the UK FE library sector, this supersedes some of the other quality framework toolkits which were previously employed in order to audit and measure performance. The FE library sector, like other academic library environments, has been subject to great change over recent years, and subsequently quality assurance and performance measurement tools and instruments have tended to change and develop at the same time. As a result it is difficult to establish a significant time series for those member libraries involved, although the current survey does now appear to be robust and is very well developed in that it has established sector-wide performance and impact indicators for the first time.

---

[4] http://www.caul.edu.au/.

[5] http://www.colric.org.uk/.

Similar usage statistics are compiled by the Chartered Institute of Public Finance and Accountancy (CIPFA)[6] for public libraries in the United Kingdom. CIPFA submissions consist of detailed spreadsheets, compiled by each public library service and include a series of usage and operational statistics such as book issues across different reader categories, number of staff, number of computers, time taken to satisfy requests, number of telephone and email enquiries received, and financial data. Like the CoLRIC return, the CIPFA survey also asks for derived statistics such as visits income per 1000 population, staff per 1000 population, etc. Both sets of returns are very thorough and effectively become very useful management information. Although they are both ultimately returned as usage figures, the derived nature of some of the statistics can start to indicate performance against targets, objectives, and outcomes and are subsequently used as performance indicators.

For public libraries in the United States the Institute of Museum and Library Services (IMLS)[7] collects nationwide descriptive statistics on all public libraries along with those for state libraries. These statistics are similar to those returned to CIPFA in the United Kingdom and again include usage statistics as well as operational statistics such as number of books, number of computer terminals, number of staff members, etc. IMLS covers returns for 9000 public libraries, with approximately 17,000 individual public library branches along with the 50 state libraries. IMLS works alongside the National Centre for Education Statistics, responsible for the statistical data collection of the US university libraries, which allows for a very significant and consistent return of library statistics and metrics across both the public and academic library sectors in the United States.

The previous examples should demonstrate that statistical returning within library and information services and sectors is indeed massively and commonly practiced. The metrics available to librarians and library administrators can be easily collected and collated and presented to tell the story about how the library is operating. There is of course some debate as to whether the statistics alone can demonstrate how the library is performing, but it remains the case that returning statistics and metrical measures is a fundamental element of library quality management. Over the last 20 or 30 years the digital information revolution which has occurred in society as a whole has had a huge impact on library and information

[6] http://www.cipfa.org.uk/.

[7] http://www.imls.gov/.

service provision. Along with the customer service culture which libraries now operate within, service expectations of library users have changed significantly, and while electronic and digital resource usage features heavily in all of the previous examples of statistical returns and surveys, there is a school of thought that the usage statistics and metrics associated with e-resource usage should be treated separately from other library service usage.

6.3 STATISTICAL MEASURES FOR E-RESOURCES

As mentioned in the previous chapter, Crawford, a recognised and credible commentator on library performance and quality differentiates between the evaluation of general library services and electronic library services and suggests that access to resources which are leased or licensed needs to be counted separately and treated differently with regard to their evaluation (Crawford, 2006, p. 135). However, there is a growing realisation across all library sectors that libraries need to focus more on their communities than their collections and that libraries are no longer primarily defined by the printed collections that they own, but how they, as services provide value to their users. Subsequently, the focus for collections has become more and more about access, rather than ownership, meaning that the measuring of usage of resources needs to be comprehensive and present a true picture of how a library's resources are being used, whether they are owned, borrowed, leased, or licensed.

Since the turn of the century electronic resource provision and usage, particularly e-journals and e-books have grown exponentially. For higher education and research libraries spending on e-resource, acquisition has accounted for the majority of the information resources budget for many years now, and the metrics generated for e-resource searches and downloads suggest far greater usage that statistics provided for issues and returns of printed resources. E-resource usage figures continue to increase and the business and management of e-resources has become a whole specialist discipline within librarianship. Similar trends are being experienced in all library sectors as publishers provide more and more access to journals and books in electronic formats and in a competitive manner through aggregated 'bundles' and packages. Accordingly, quantitative methods for measuring usage and potential impact of electronic and digital resources have become common practice.

There are some initiatives that have been implemented to assist in the growing electronic library resources environment. COUNTER (Counting

Online Usage of Networked Electronic Resources)[8] was launched in 2002 as an international initiative serving librarians, publishers, and aggregators by setting standards to facilitate the recording and reporting of online usage statistics in a consistent format. COUNTER uses a code of practice to do this and this now extends to e-journals, e-books, databases, and reference works. Many publishers and content vendors now ensure that they are COUNTER compliant, which allows for consistency across sectors and institutions. Similarly, the Journal Usage Statistics Portal (JUSP)[9] provides a service to libraries in the United Kingdom whereby an individual library's journal collection statistics are collected and aggregated and data is presented back to the library to help understand how journal content is actually used. Such data, once collected can help the e-resource manager or library administrator to see which journals or which packages are most used and to analyse trends in order to make decisions with regard to managing their electronic subscriptions. The work of COUNTER and JUSP has been borne out of and has subsequently assisted the ever increasing electronic library resource environment. They allow for libraries to quantitatively measure the usage of their scholarly material which in turn can aid decision making from a collections perspective.

6.4 LIBRARY ANALYTICS AND METRICS

The growing interest in library data and analytics sits very neatly within this broader discussion around quantitative measures. We can see already in this chapter that libraries are in the habit of collecting statistics and data for informing all elements of their service. The variety and scope of data collected and generated by libraries is significant: transactional data on catalogues searches, item checkouts, logins to e-resources, statistics on space, statistics on satisfaction, etc. The application of this data is equally varied and overlapping including management functions (collections development), impact (benchmarking, improving learner outcomes), and improving services (Showers, 2015a, 2015b, xxvi). Using such data to demonstrate impact and value and to understand how outcomes are being met starts to move these particular quantitative measures into the realms of analytics.

---

[8] www.projectcounter.org/about.html.

[9] https://www.jusp.mimas.ac.uk/about/.

6.5 BIBLIOMETRICS

It seems appropriate to briefly mention bibliometrics whilst discussing analytics and metrics, although technically bibliometrics does not concern itself with a library's performance. A field of informetrics, 'the study of quantitative aspects of information', bibliometrics was first referred to in a paper published by Alan Pritchard in 1969, in which he defined the term as "the application of mathematics and statistical methods to books and other media of communication" (Pritchard, 1969, p. 348).

Nowadays bibliometrics comprises of a set of quantitative methods used to analyse the impact of academic literature and can be used across any academic discipline. Citation analysis and content analysis are the two most commonly used bibliometric tools. Citation analysis, in brief involves examining how many times an individual article is cited and referred to and an analysis on its ultimate academic impact. Such work was traditionally done manually, often by a librarian, but over recent years automated citation indexes have emerged and are often made available by publishers and content aggregators as complementary services. For example, Thompson Reuters' Web of Science service provides a comprehensive set of citation indexes including the Science Citation Index, the Social Science Citation Index, and the Arts and Humanities Citation Index which can then be broken down into smaller specialist subset indexes. The publishing giant Elsevier promotes its Scopus product as an abstract and citation database containing 21,000 journal titles from over 5000 publishers and including citation details and analysis. The growth of automated bibliometrics has also resulted in the development of new professional roles, with many research and university libraries, particularly in the United States now requiring a bibliometrician to conduct and oversee such work for their library and their institution. Data from citation indexes can be analysed to determine the popularity and impact of specific articles and journals. This in turn can assist the management of a library's resources as well as providing potential quantitative evidence of the value and impact of the collections that the library provides access to.

6.6 ALTMETRICS

The most recent addition to the toolkit of quantitative measures for demonstrating impact is that of 'Alternative metrics' or 'Altmetrics'.

Like bibliometrics, altmetrics originates from the need to demonstrate the impact of scientific scholarship and publishing, but altmetrics does not rely exclusively on the citation as the tool for its measurement. Instead altmetrics takes into account the 21st-century digital environment in which "the growing pervasiveness of the Web is creating an environment in which scholars and other users create new kinds of tracks that reveal once-invisible scholarly activities" (Priem, 2014, p. 264). Altmetrics dismisses that bibliographic citation analysis is the only way of demonstrating academic value and that web-based social media tools such as reference management services, blogs and microblogs, and bookmarking services are becoming increasingly in the dissemination of scholarship across all disciplines.

6.7 QUESTIONNAIRES AND SURVEYS

As identified before, many library statistics can be collected and collated internally either by simply returning fixed data (number of staff, budget figures, etc.) or by counting and monitoring how many occurrences there are of a particular type of item, transaction, visit, etc. Another, perhaps more sophisticated method of extracting quantitative data about a library and information service is that of the survey. Surveys can allow the library administrator to further evaluate the usage of the library service by asking the users of the library about their usage, rather than simply counting and monitoring usage through statistical returns or observation.

Quantitative survey methods, through the use of structured and often closed questions can report on the views of many library users and present a critical mass of opinion on outcomes such as levels of satisfaction with a service, or perhaps targeted element of service such as study space, opening hours, accessibility, etc. Questionnaires can also report on usage patterns by asking users how often they visit the library or access a particular service. A well-designed quantitative library survey will generate clear numerical answers to the questions posed, which by their nature are regarded as scientific and objectively achieved. Surveys are a great way of reaching a metric or statistic as a tool for demonstrating usage patterns or for validating trends through breadth of data (i.e. x% of library users are satisfied with services, x% of library users feel that the library should be open for longer hours).

Satisfaction surveys, in particular, are very well used by library services across all sectors. Hernon and Whitman (2001) suggest that satisfaction with a library service occurs when the customer is content with their [library] experience as compared to other, similar experiences. Being able to demonstrate satisfaction with a service allows the library some reassurance that customer expectations are being met (or even exceeded). Similarly, evaluation through surveying customers also allows the library to see where they are falling short of meeting their customers' expectations and can result in setting actions for service improvement and development.

In some instances it might be possible to survey a group of library users in its entirety. This would apply in a small special library, a commercial research library, or a private law library, for example, where the library administrator has access to all active library users. In larger organisations, including academic, public, and hospital libraries this is usually not possible, unless trying to target specific user groups to survey them about a particular issue (e.g. users with disabilities, a particular clinical role, etc.). For most larger library and information services, surveys are conducted through a sampling method, otherwise known as collecting inferential statistics, which uses a sample group of users, representative of the user population as a whole. Samples are chosen randomly, but there are different ways in which this can be achieved. For example, simple random sampling means that each member of the population (of library users) has an equal chance of being chosen. This supposes that a sampling frame is being used, which simply speaking is a list of all the entire population of active library users. There are also more structured approaches to random sampling and indeed there are some methods of nonrandom sampling. The nonrandom methods are very likely to be used in library and information services, where time for administration is scarce and includes accidental sampling (i.e. whoever is available) and quota sampling or purposive sampling, both of which involve choosing a sample based on a particular characteristic (age, ethnicity, gender, etc.).

Whilst sample size is important, representation of library users also needs to be considered, and library administrators often work on strategies to ensure representative responses when conducting surveys. Consideration also needs to be given to the design and administration of a questionnaire and this includes the types of questions asked (i.e. whether the questions are closed enough to generate significantly statistical data, use of Likert scales, etc.), length of survey, timing of the survey, and techniques for engaging users to complete the survey. John Crawford (2000) provides a lot of practical advice and guidance on how to plan, implement, and analyse surveys. One of his key suggestions is that of providing feedback to users on what happens as a result of conducting the survey. This is important when engaging library users in any form of performance measurement and evaluation but is particularly important with a survey because of the critical mass of the library user population engaged in the survey.

Quantitative data and statistics are easy to generate and collect, and surveys can be a straightforward way of engaging with the library customer and obtaining evaluative information from them. Traditionally library and information services looked to these methods as a means of performance measurement, and especially as a means of regular accountability to their respective stakeholders. However, in attempting to measure all services provided by libraries in this way 'there is a danger that with the imposition of lots of quality and performance accreditation processes, quality measures can turn into box ticking, statistics generation and form filling exercises' (Rowley, 2005, p. 509).

Any surveys, whether they are satisfaction surveys or perception surveys are unable to really quantify value and impact of service and they are often criticised as a performance measurement because of this. This however seems a bit unfair, as there are far more instruments available in the library administrators toolkit with which value and impact might be demonstrated, and the point where surveys are able to contribute to this is where the questions are posed to the user which require free text, anecdotal, or qualitative responses. Such a question is often left to the end of a survey (e.g. *Do you have any other comments? What are your favourite things about the library? What would you improve in the library?*).

Crawford (2006, p. 42) suggests that "qualitative research is often seen as an addition to quantitative methods as a means of getting an understanding of the attitudes that inform the statistics." Perhaps this is why the open-ended questions are left until the end of the survey, but the information which library administrators receive from these anecdotes and comments that can often prove as useful as the quantitative survey data itself.

6.8 VALUE FOR MONEY

A recent development in assessing the impact of public libraries in the United Kingdom has seen a movement to ascertain the economic value that they provide. Demonstrating the 'value' of a library service through 'value for money' or 'return on investment' draws heavily on the metrics and quantitative measures available. McMenemy (2009) discusses how measuring outputs alongside the measurement of economic impacts should provide evidence of value for money, but also introduces the system of contingent valuation, which aims to survey users as well as nonusers in assessing a public library's economic value. He draws upon the work of Aabo and Audunsen (2002) who discuss in greater detail the rational choice theory behind contingent evaluation in that individuals must anticipate the outcomes of alternative course of action and calculate that which will be best for them.

Contingent valuation involves constructing a market by interviewing potential users of that market (or service). It uses a mechanism for eliciting value from the respondent and takes into account the respondent's socioeconomic characteristics, attitudes, and behaviours towards the service (or commodity). Contingent valuation is key to understanding how measuring the value and impact of a public service can really work, as it can be used for measuring the values that nonusers place on a library service, something that more traditional quantitative and qualitative measures cannot do. For example, "a person who does not use the public library will have no opinion on the quality of its collections, but they may still place value on the public library's collections in terms of its worth to society" (McMenemy, 2009, p. 156). The method has been used to demonstrate return on investment for every pound/dollar spent on a public library service and McMenemy provides a few examples of this with varying results, for example, a recent use of the methodology at the British Library suggested that for every £1.00 spent on the service, a return of £4.00 is generated (Pung, Clarke, & Patten, 2004). Using contingent valuation as part of a methodology for assessing and measuring value of a public library service would appear to be fundamental to any such study and needs to be explored further.

The financial value of libraries is often questioned, most usually by key stakeholders responsible for resourcing and funding the library service. Therefore 'impact' can be assessed with 'value' in mind.

Where measurement and evaluation clearly demonstrate success against anticipated outcomes, this can suggest an added 'value' of the library service to the user or stakeholder. Evaluation can invariably demonstrate both impact (i.e. where there is a benefit or a change as a result of intervention in trying to achieve an outcome) and value (i.e. the perceived benefit to the user and stakeholder). For this reason 'impact assessment' discussions often include those around libraries demonstrating 'Return on Investment', which allows a library to quantify and demonstrate the library's economic value to its stakeholders.

A great example of this is the 'Return on Investment' study done as part of the aforementioned LibValue project:

> For every euro or dollar or yen spent on the library, the university receives euros or dollars or yen back in the form of additional grants, income or donations, or long term value to the community from an educated workforce, more productive faculty and more successful students

> *(Tenopir, 2010, p. 40)*

The main focus of the LibValue programme is to illustrate return on investment and a progress report suggest that the strands of the programme are producing such outcomes, although in some instances, such as the strand looking at the 'Value of library instructional services to teaching and learning' demonstrate a lot of what the project calls 'implied value', in that respondents tend to acknowledge the benefit of using library resources in terms of 'time saved' and also report 'improvement in their students work as a result of using library resources' (Tenopir & Fleming-May, 2011).

It is evident from the literature that during the period from 2005 to 2010, being able to demonstrate return on investment in library resources, particularly with regard to its impact on research, was becoming increasingly important. This extended not just to the major US academic research libraries, but further field to Europe and also to the publishers and aggregators of electronic library resources (Luther, 2008). An insightful case study to come from this period is that of the University of Illinois at Urbana-Champaign and a piece of research into return on investment which they undertook with the publisher Elsevier. Again, Carol Tenopir is involved with this case study as it was clearly linked to (although not part of) the LibValue programme. The objective of the research was to be able to demonstrate that investment into digital and electronic library resources generates higher usage and ultimately higher quality research output. Being able to demonstrate such an impact is clearly a significant instrument when libraries come to set business cases for University funding. Luther, herself a consultant to Elsevier, discusses how the case study which effectively demonstrates a return on investment paves the way for academic libraries to negotiate with their own institutions. Of course, being able to demonstrate that library usage has such a positive outcome and a positive impact on research and scholarship, and therefore the potential for the institution to bring in even more funding from an increase in research grants, is to be celebrated.

CHAPTER SEVEN

Qualitative Methods for Performance Measurement

Qualitative and quantitative research methods are often dealt with separately and along with this division there is an unwritten hierarchy in research circles that quantitative research is considered to be more rigorous, more reliable, and more precise (Berg, 2009, p. 2). This is perhaps one of the reasons why the 'user' focus of library and information services being at the heart of quality and performance measurement was not always as strong as it might have been. Traditionally, librarians, wishing to demonstrate rigour in their measures tended to favour the quantitative approaches as favoured by other social scientists. However with emergence of the importance of the library user, methods need to be deployed which "attempt to understand behaviour and institutions by getting to know the persons involved and their values, rituals, symbols, beliefs, and emotions" (Nachimas & Worth-Nachimas, 2008, p. 257). In other words, the measures that the modern day library administrator requires need to be meaningful and in today's library and information environment that means that they need to be able to describe the value and the impact that the library has on the individual users and communities and statistics alone, with no meaningful context cannot do this.

"Quantitative methodology assumes the objective reality of social facts, where qualitative assumes social constructions of reality" (Gorman & Clayton, 2005, p. 24). This quotation suggests that where the quantitative data obtained through survey questions and statistical returns presents us with definitive factual information (i.e. x number of book issues, $x\%$ of satisfied users, etc.) qualitative methods will help to validate those facts through 'real life' examples. This might take the form of a user expressing satisfaction or dissatisfaction with a service. Qualitative methods for performance measurement in library and information services are often more revealing when they are based on direct contact with library users. Indeed, such direct contact can help immensely to validate quantitative findings. Qualitative methods encourage observation, discussion, and reflection and can help the library administrator to identify issues and problems and get to the details of such situations, or conversely can help to demonstrate the impact and value that a library service has on its users. There are several basic as well as more sophisticated qualitative methods available to library administrators and these can be used separately or collective to aid the quality and performance measurement processes as well as for validating any quantitative data and management information available.

7.1 FOCUS GROUPS

Focus group interviews typically have five characteristics or features. These characteristics relate to the ingredients of a focus group: (1) people, who (2) possess certain characteristics, (3) provide qualitative data (4) in a focused discussion (5) to help understand the topic of interest.

(Krueger & Casey, 2009, p. 6)

The focus group is a well-established qualitative method used in the social sciences. A focus group is designed to generate broad discussion amongst participants (in this case library users) which then narrows down to focus on particular key issues. The role of the facilitator in these situations is very important in encouraging positive discussion without actually directing or controlling the flow of the discussion.

Focus groups had originally been popular in the commercial world amongst market researchers but have since become an acceptable method for academic research. Once this was the case, the focus became less about consumer products and more about issues such as community, education, social issues, and public policy (Morgan, 1997). Whilst focus groups are still very widely used in the market research world, so too are they in research environments. Indeed, focus groups should encourage discussion and reflection and well-constructed questioning can reveal deep and focused data, which is why this has become a standard method for data capture in social science research (Bloor, Frankland, Thomas, & Robson, 2002).

Where this lends itself to library and information services as a performance measurement method is in its discussion and reflection activity. Groups of service users, brought together by a common characteristic, that of using the same library service, can often go into far more detail of a current issue or situation based on their own observations and experiences (e.g. relevance of book stock, accessibility, opening hours, staff expertise, and support) and their focused discussions can help to validate or triangulate data obtained through quantitative methods such as surveys. Focus groups need to be objectively facilitated and similarly, need to be facilitated with objectives in mind. Trying to expand upon quantitative findings can be one such objective.

Used in isolation and without any objectives, focus groups can sometimes become 'moaning sessions' for those participating. For this reason, it is important that the facilitator is skilled and focused and is able to lead the discussion effectively.

Whilst the focus group is grounded firmly within a research methodology, many library administrators take the format and adapt it according to their needs as a performance measurement tool. The format is sometimes referred to by another name such as 'library user group' or 'library critical friends group' in order to convey what the group represents to the user, but the underpinning scope and remit of such a group is often that of a focus group.

7.2 INTERVIEWS

Where the focus group is designed to provoke deep qualitative discussion, the interview is used to gain an in-depth understanding of an individual's perceptions or to get a deeper understanding of the thoughts, ideas, and opinions of the subject being interviewed. Bloor and Wood (2006, p. 105) define the interview as "the elicitation of research data through the questioning of respondents" and go onto to suggest that interviews can sit in both methodological frameworks. Quantitative interviews are structured in their nature, have a semiformal character, and are conducted in surveys using a standardised interview schedule. The qualitative interview, however, is semistructured and takes a more conversational and reflective approach, shaped by the interviewer's interest and rationale for the research along with enabling themes and topics to emerge from the interview itself.

Pickard (2006, p. 172) suggests that in library and information research, interviews are more widely used when we are seeking qualitative, descriptive, in-depth data which is specific to an individual and when the nature of the data is too difficult to be asked and answered easily.

Qualitative interviews can often be used to complement focus group activity. For example, a group of active library users may be brought together in a focus group to discuss broad quality themes, and the librarian conducting the focus group may decide that some of the participants might have more to contribute and might consider inviting them for a deeper discussion in the form of a research interview in order to further into the thoughts and perceptions of those individual users. Crawford (2006, p. 50) describes the advantages of using interviews as a research or performance measurement technique and explains how interviews provide a friendlier and more personal and inclusive technique which might appeal to those who are reluctant to take part in group events or subjects who cannot easily take part in other discursive methods (e.g. children, subjects with language barriers, etc.).

There are two distinct types of interview: the structured interview which asks the interviewee a series of preestablished questions with a limited set of response categories; and the unstructured interview where only the general subject area is predetermined and gives lots of scope and opportunity for the person being interviewed to express themselves. In between these two interview types is the semistructured interview where the interviewer will probably refer to a list of themes and topics and will have predetermined, but open-ended questions, which still allow the respondent to think and reflect deeply.

All these types of interview require sound interviewing skills of the researcher or library administrator and particularly when using unstructured or semistructured interviews as a qualitative measure. The ability to compose and ask the right questions alongside making use of active listening skills is all important with this particular method.

Focus group and interviews are common qualitative research and performance measurement methods and are widely used by library and information practitioners, as it allows questions to be asked about service, perception, and satisfaction, which in turn can provide deep, experiential data on which to make decisions about service levels and performance and on potential developments and improvements. These discursive approaches allow the library administrator to ask questions about the potential value and impact that the library and information service has on its users.

In addition, there are several other, slightly less intrusive, qualitative techniques at the disposal of the library administrator.

7.3 SUGGESTION BOXES/COMMENTS SCHEMES/ EVALUATIONS

It could certainly be argued that the commonly used 'suggestion box', possibly found in all libraries is not technically a performance measurement tool or technique, but it is a means of asking questions of your library users and finding out what they think. Participating in focus groups or interviews may well be outside the comfort zone of many users, but a proactive approach to seeking feedback through comments or suggestion schemes and in the evaluation of specific elements of support or service (i.e. skills sessions or enquiry service) can bring about rich qualitative data as well as genuine suggestions for improvement.

Such initiatives are regarded as very effective user engagement methods and where a library publicises and promotes such schemes and encourages comments and feedback they will often find that library users are happy and willing to make use of such platforms (especially if they see actions and outcomes from their suggestions).

As a performance measurement tool, feedback and comments schemes allow the library administrator to spot trends, issues, and concerns (e.g. it might be that a particular member of staff is continually being praised or acknowledged, or it may be multiple complaints about the same facility or electronic resource). This information often validates and therefore complements data retrieved form the other performance measurement methods already discussed (i.e. focus groups, interviews, surveys, etc.).

7.4 OBSERVATION

According to Crawford (2006, p. 51) observation as a qualitative technique is used relatively little in libraries. The technique comprises of literally observing how the users of the library service use their library service and focuses on user behaviours. Observation can be done in a structured fashion, where the observer is looking out for particular behaviours and activities (e.g. use of computers or quiet study space) or in a more unstructured way where the observer records any behaviour or event taking place in the library which is relevant to the performance being measured.

Again, as with feedback and comments schemes, it could be argued that observation in its true form does not really contribute to measuring the performance of a library, but it does present the library administrator with more data about users (in particular their behaviours) which might validate or triangulate data from elsewhere (i.e. observations of users accessing electronic library resources correlating with increased e-resource usage). Markless and Streatfield (2006, p. 96) argue strongly that it is a shame that observation is not used more in libraries as it is "a great way to develop ideas about how people use information, how library systems and services can be improved to how people can improve their teaching, training or interaction with service users."

Observation as a stand-alone method does not appear to be widely used within library and information services, but there is currently a growing interest in 'user experience' (UX) in libraries, which is discussed later and makes use of specific forms of observation as a fundamental part of its method.

7.5 REFLECTIVE JOURNALS AND DIARIES

Using reflective logs or participant diaries is more of a qualitative research method than a tool for performance measurement of libraries. However, they should still be considered when looking at qualitative methods for performance measurement as they are useful for confirming and validating data retrieved from other methods. That is they can provide anecdotal evidence of the findings of surveys or usage statistics, or further discussion to add to the findings of a focus group. As both a research method and a performance measure reflective diaries and logs come in for quite a lot of criticism. Slater (1990) regards them as recorded self-observations and as such suggests that they are too subjective to be effective. However, in her book *Research Methods in Information* Pickard suggest that they are unfortunately, largely overlooked and argues that they can be of use by offering insight into the behaviour, feelings, and thoughts of those taking part (Pickard, 2006, p. 211). They have recently become a more accepted method within user experience initiatives in libraries and this is elaborated upon in a later section.

7.6 BENCHMARKING

Benchmarking is a very interesting method and is another that is quite often overlooked when discussing performance measurement in libraries. Peter Brophy dedicates an excellent chapter to benchmarking in his book *Measuring Library Performance* and suggests that within any library sector the services offered share many common characteristics and therefore it can be very useful to compare the performance of one library with others. He goes on to say that it can also be used to make internal comparisons between branches, departments, or sections (Brophy, 2006, p. 147).

Libraries are well placed to compare themselves with each other in that they share so many similarities and many library and information procedures and provisions are similar to one another (i.e. counting users, square metres of library space, cataloguing, classification, print items, electronic resources, etc.). It is not uncommon for libraries to compare themselves with other similar libraries within their sector or their benchmark group, and this is helped in that many libraries are publicly funded and not constrained by considerations of commercial confidentiality as is the case in many corporate organisations.

For these reasons libraries tend to use benchmarking as a quality procedure which includes performance measurement or certainly performance comparisons. One of the key considerations when doing benchmarking exercises is for the library to be focused as to what it is benchmarking and what it hopes to achieve. Process benchmarking is often treated differently to usage benchmarking, the former being an exercise to compare processes with a view to process improvement, and the latter focusing on quantitative data to see if there are trends or differences with regard to library outputs. The organisations mentioned in the first part of this chapter, which are responsible for gathering statistics in their respective sectors (i.e. CIPFA and IMLS for public libraries, SCONUL and ARL for academic libraries) all allow for their member institutions to compare, and therefore benchmark their usage statistics.

7.7 USER EXPERIENCE (UX)

User Experience (UX) in libraries involves a suite of techniques based around first understanding and then improving the experience that users have when using libraries. One of the fundamental principles of UX is that it uses ethnographic methods to achieve this. Ethnography in libraries is not particularly new and there exists a wealth of excellent and interesting case studies, largely from the United States of highly successful applications of ethnographic and anthropological studies in libraries (Delcore et al., 2009; Duke & Asher, 2012; Foster & Gibbons, 2007; Suarez, 2007; White, 2009). In all instances ethnographic techniques are used to observe and then further inform potential developments in many aspects of library and information services and activity (e.g. collection management, resource discovery, information-seeking behaviour, library instruction, space planning, etc.).

In a library and information setting, ethnography provides 'a way of studying cultures through observation, participation and other qualitative techniques with a view to better understanding the subject's point of view and experience of the world' (Priestner, 2015). Until recently, UX was largely applied by libraries to the design and usability of websites and systems interfaces, but more recently academic libraries have begun to show willingness to apply UX in a broader approach and now increasingly use ethnographic methodologies when exploring the user experience in their physical spaces (Bryant, Matthews, & Walton, 2009). Nowadays, UX in libraries effectively makes use of these ethnographic approaches in order to see how library users actually use the resources, services, and spaces provided by the library, which in turn can contribute to service improvement and development. UX goes beyond the quantitative measures, with a view to obtaining a more illuminating and complex picture of user behaviour and user need.

Priestner and Borg (2016) discuss some of the reasons as to why UX has recently become popular as a research method and suggest that it is in part a response to the demand to the traditional quantitative measures used by libraries (e.g. statistics on footfall, holdings, loans, renewals, database use, downloads, views, social media followers) don't reveal anything about the success of the interaction, the experience of the user, and ultimately the value or impact that the library use has on the user. They suggest that the focus in UK higher education on 'student experience' has led library managers and administrators to look at how and why library users use libraries in the way that they do (as opposed to the ways in which librarians would have them use them) in order to better understand what users want from libraries.

With the intended end result of using UX as a research method being service improvement and development, it needs to be considered alongside other library performance measurement tools and techniques, and in effect draws upon a suite of qualitative methods, some already covered in this chapter in order to do this. Examples of UX methods include observation of user movement in the library (to see where users naturally physically travel to within their library spaces as opposed to where the librarians think they travel to), observation of activity within given spaces (to see how users naturally behave in demarked spaces and environments), walking though library spaces with users to observe and discuss how they use the library, focused discussion with library users about what works for them and what doesn't, diaries and reflective exercises about users' experience of the library, observation of alternative library or service-oriented spaces, directed storytelling, unstructured interviews, photo studies, cognitive mapping, etc.

By researching through using one or more of these methods, library managers are able to generate significant and large quantities of data which then needs to be critiqued and analysed. Ramsden (2016) discusses how data from UX projects needs to be effectively collected and analysed, but essentially there needs to be a coding process and a critical standpoint needs to be assumed. It is important not to lose sight of the aim of UX is to look at the service wholly from a user perspective (as opposed to a financial or political perspective).

One of the reasons why UX is a relatively new performance measurement method for libraries is that traditionally the library space (design, layout, access, practicality of use, etc.) was not really considered when addressing performance. The focus was rather more on the quantitative and statistical measures mentioned earlier, and the exploration of user behaviours within library spaces was not regarded as being part of any such measures. With 'experience' now being all important, this is no longer the case and due to its ethnographic nature, UX is very well placed to address this. UX is therefore being increasingly used to inform the 'design' of library services with the user at the heart of the decision making and the intended outcome being to improve the quality of the library for the benefit of the user, through improved design.

Design suggests an intentional attempt to create, and the expression of some type of vision, rather than an arbitrary or unintentional occurrence
(Dent-Goodman, 2011, pp. 111–112)

The notion of 'design' is a key one within UX. The delivery of high-quality, high-performing library services is the aim of every library manager and effective services need to be 'designed'. Schmidt (2010) suggests librarians are quite often unknowingly involved in design, in as much as every operational management decision (e.g. about loan periods, where to house a collection, how to create access to a collection, introducing new services, etc.) are all decisions about the design of the library service. What UX does is ensure that the users' behaviours, use, and expectation of the library service are behind any such decisions.

Ultimately UX is about the quality and the performance of service design of libraries and presents its own toolkit of qualitative methods through which this can be measured. Bell (2010) states that UX can extend to every touch point which the library creates where the user or community connects with the library's human or material resources, both physically or virtually. He also suggests that UX starts with the most basic of elements, the core values of the library service (Bell, 2010, pp. 6–7). This point assumes that most (if not all) libraries share common values about equitable access to quality resources and ensuring that users of the library have a highly positive experience. As we have already suggested the modern day 21st-century library does indeed focus itself on the user or customer, but this was not always the case, which is why UX is relatively newcomer to the suite of qualitative methods used by library administrators to measure performance.

Through placing the user at the heart of the method, UX really harnesses the concept of the library user as the customer and really focuses on the quality of their experience. UX seeks to identify how the library has a positive impact on the user by finding out exactly how the user interacts and uses the library, what the user values about the library, and then playing to those strengths.

CHAPTER EIGHT

Mixed Methods for Performance Measurement

Mixed methods, in any sphere of social science research refers to the mix of both quantitative and qualitative methods used, usually resulting in a robust performance measurement tool where statistics and metrics are used to validate the qualitative findings derived from other channels (e.g. where library usage statistics might be used alongside qualitative or anecdotal data about how a library is used).

There are several recognised mixed method approaches which are used by library and information services and the final part of this chapter will provide a brief introduction to them.

8.1 QUALITY FRAMEWORKS

The quality framework is a mixed method approach carried out in a standard form across a whole sector or a group of institutions in order to compare and benchmark against each other. Comparing and benchmarking against similar institutions in the library and information sector is often used in order to justify business cases or increases in investment in libraries, although this is often done using exclusively statistical data. However, the true quality framework uses both standardised quantitative and qualitative data to report local performance and to share and compare performance within a wider (sectoral) context. Two such quality frameworks used in the United Kingdom are the CoLRIC[1] framework used in the library and information services at colleges of further education and the NHS quality framework[2] used to evaluate the performance of health and medical libraries.

---

[1] http://www.colric.org.uk/.

[2] http://www.libraryservices.nhs.uk/forlibrarystaff/lqaf/.

Libraries and Key Performance Indicators
http://dx.doi.org/10.1016/B978-0-08-100227-8.00008-X

8.2 ANNUAL REPORTING

Whilst not technically a mixed method approach to performance measurement, the library service annual report is a form reporting back to the parent institution on progress and development and this is often done against targets and objectives. You are unlikely to find too much by the way of literature or analysis on 'annual reports', but most library and information services will habitually produce them (often at the end of a financial or academic year cycle), often reluctantly as a necessary evil in order to comply with corporate directives. However, if used effectively, annual reports can be a useful performance check and an opportunity for libraries to report back on how well (or not) they have done during the previous 12 months with regards to achieving against the objectives and targets that they might have set or been set for them. There has been much discussion in the previous chapters about libraries needing to be clear about their intended outcomes if they are ever going to truly be able to measure their impact and value. I would suggest that the setting of strategic objectives and associated targets (often metrical) go some way to presenting this clarity with regard to intended outcomes, which means that the annual report starts to become a powerful performance measurement reporting tool. The annual report is a great opportunity to present the library's performance both in numbers and in a contextual format where narrative is used to explain what the numbers actually mean.

Many libraries use their annual report to report back their annual usage statistics (e.g. number of visits to the library, number of books issued, number of electronic downloads, number of orientation sessions), satisfaction measures (e.g. percentage of satisfied customers as per the library survey, percentage of users satisfied with orientation measures), and cost analyses (e.g. cost per head of library usage, spend per library user, etc.). All of this data is arbitrary unless presented in some context. That is to say that rather than simply presenting the metrics as an increase or a decrease from the year before they would become more meaningful if presented as a measure of how well the library was performing against a particular target associated with a strategic objective or overall outcome. At this point the metrics presented become 'indicators' of performance against a predetermined outcome, objective, or target.

Having said this, if the annual report is to be used as a true mixed method approach to reporting on library performance the annual production of this report should not be the only time that the statistics involved are collated and analysed. Statistics in these instances need to be obtained and scrutinised regularly in order to assess performance and to allow library managers to make informed decisions based on this. At this juncture the statistics in question have become some sort of performance or result indicator, which is the theme of the next chapter.

8.3 BALANCED SCORECARDS

The Balanced Scorecard (BCS) is a popular business management tool used by organisations which wish to evaluate the performance of different aspects of the business and report back holistically in order to demonstrate interdependencies. It is a widely used strategic performance management framework that allows organisation to identify, manage, and measure their strategic objectives (Marr, 2015a, 2015b, p. 46).

The Balanced Scorecard was developed in the early 1990s by Dr. Robert Kaplan and Dr. David Norton when they noticed that most companies measured their performance through exclusively financial measures. On the basis that financial performance only relates to how a company had performed in the past, they do not tell a business leader much about where the business is headed in the future. Kaplan and Norton suggested that in isolation, financial measures are not particularly 'balanced' or insightful with regard to setting strategy and that a more balanced method which takes into account non-financial objectives and activities, such as customer experience, internal processes, and staff motivation would be more desirable (Kaplan & Norton, 1996). The four perspectives of the original balanced Scorecard are as follows:

- *Financial* – focus on the performance with regard to the financial objectives of an organisation (e.g. how much profit, return on investment, etc.)
- *Customer* – focus on performance and quality from the point of view of the customer (e.g. customer satisfaction or experience)
- *Internal processes* – focus on internal operational goals and objectives and key processes required to deliver the customer objectives
- *Learning and growth* – focus on staff and employee performance with regard to staff skills, training, organisational culture, and leadership

Through focusing on these four perspectives the Balanced Scorecard considers both internal processes and external outcomes in order to look at continuous improvement and positive results. David Parmenter (2010) champions the balanced scorecard as a holistic method of measuring performance but also suggests two further perspectives to be considered alongside those identified by Kaplan and Norton above. These are as follows:

- *Environment/community* – focus on where the institution sits within the community or region and the impact it has on its locality
- *Employee satisfaction* – focus retention of key staff, recognition and reward, staff motivation

By measuring performance against either the four or six perspectives of the balanced scorecard an organisation's leaders can measure, analyse, and improve all of them together, therefore making for a more stable and strategically sound performance measurement platform.

The balanced scorecard was initially considered to be an instrument for the private (for-profit) sector, but Kaplan himself suggested that its "potential to improve the management of public sector organisation is even greater" (Kaplan, 1999, p. 1). Several commentators went on to argue that it was not quite so easy to transfer the balanced scorecard approach into the public sector due to the multiplicity of customers and stakeholders in the public sector (Greatbanks & Tapp, 2001) and that the framework needed to be changed in order to capture their mission-driven nature, placing more emphasis in accountability and results in meeting user expectations for public services and products (Rohm, 2004).

Having said this, many libraries have now adopted a balanced scorecard approach, and a recent review of this practice found that the key drivers for using such an approach was to improve library management, both strategically and operationally (De La Mano & Creaser, 2014). This research showed that considerable support was required in order to develop balanced scorecard frameworks for libraries and that one of the most challenging things was developing and selecting meaningful and appropriate performance indicators and key performance indicators. For library and information services the balanced scorecard allows the library to translate the organisation's strategic objectives (its mission and overall strategy) into a coherent set of measures that reflect its specific goals and targets. An effective and transparent scorecard will enable an observer to deduce the organisation's strategy, and how well it is performing against it, at a glance (Corrall, 2000).

The balanced scorecard offers a robust 'mixed method' approach for libraries to measure performance and quality and as such the framework can make use of qualitative evidence as well as metrics, but key performance indicators play a crucial role in the effective execution of a balanced scorecard.

CHAPTER NINE

An Overview of Key Performance Indicators

9.1 IS A KPI NOT JUST A STATISTIC?

The previous chapters allude to the fact that the statistics collected by libraries in order to demonstrate and measure performance should be seen as indicators and should be analysed regularly throughout the planning or review cycle. As explained in the introduction to the book, one of the objectives for writing this book was to unpick what performance indicators and KPIs mean for libraries. There is very little literature on this area specifically for library and information services, nor are there any common guidelines which clearly demonstrate how library performance indicators can be developed and used. The IFLA guidelines on measuring quality in libraries (Poll & Te Boekhorst, 2007) do indeed acknowledge the need for performance indicators but their focus on performance measurement in general means that the specific details of how these should be developed and applied is missing.

Similarly, there exists an International Standard for library performance indicators (ISO 11620:2014), which now in its latest revised version includes performance indicators for both printed and electronic materials made accessible through libraries. The standard is applicable to all types of libraries and attempts to standardise the terminology used across all library sectors (i.e. for the services and resources offered by libraries) and to comprehensively list performance indicators which might be used by libraries. This is a good starting point for developing library performance indicators especially as the standard provides guidance on how to implement performance indicators where they have not already been in use (International Organisation for Standardisation, 2014). ISO 11620 is a formidable tool for library managers, and well worth consulting, but what it cannot provide is any local context for the performance indicators to operate within. The next chapters will explain why the local vision, mission, and strategy of the library are all important when attempting to measure performance and develop performance indicators.

Chapter 3 included the introduction of the concept of 'new managerialism' having affected how public services needed to become more accountable to their customers. During this period in areas other than the library sector, the quality assurance agendas started to include performance indicators as tools to measure performance and success. For example, during the 1990s (the age of new managerialism) governments all over the world became increasingly determined to make higher education more accountable to the taxpayer. In the UK higher education sector, in a bid to make universities more efficient and effective, the government began to find universities, based on their performance. Universities were expected to justify their costs through input/output performance indicator models (Johnes & Taylor, 1990). Outputs were measured through student attainments, student progression, and student employment upon leaving university (Cave, Hanney, Henkel, & Kogan, 1997). Universities' successes were judged on these types of measure and as a result the measures themselves were regarded as performance indicators. It could be argued that such measures are not helpful in addressing year-on-year developments, as if outputs are measured against inputs as performance indicators then it is necessary to wait until the outputs have been achieved, before any subsequent action or improvement can occur. Similarly, Carter, Klein, and Day (1995) discuss and analyse how the British Civil Service developed a culture of using output-based performance indicators to measure the performance of government and government departments, and to hold them to account. Such accountability is welcome, but it could be argued that using input/output-based performance indicators in this way does not generate a culture of performance measurement with the intention of service development and improvement at its heart. In order to do this, performance indicators need to be based around outcomes rather than outputs, and this certainly applies to library and information performance measurement.

As discussed in this book already, one particular tool which is continually referred to in the literature about 'evaluation of library service' is that of key performance indicators (KPIs). In the business world, KPIs are regarded as being vital for managers to understand whether their business is operating effectively and moving in the right direction. For businesses KPIs provide essential information around potential success or failure. Much of the literature about KPIs focuses on the corporate and private sectors, but KPIs can equally be applied in the public, not for profit and voluntary sectors. As long there is a line between success and failure, and varying degrees of each, with regard to the business of the organisation then KPIs are an appropriate management tool to embrace. And for this reason KPIs are highly appropriate for libraries and information services.

The International Federation of Library Associations (IFLA) guidelines are regarded as one of the definitive international guidelines for measuring quality in libraries and suggest that there is a clear need for the use of KPIs in order to assess either the library's overall performance or the quality of a specific activity or service (Poll & Te Boekhorst, 2007).

The guidelines are quite clear that they are not intended to measure the outcome (impact) of library activities. Therefore whilst the IFLA guidelines do not help us to identify how impact and value are effectively and consistently measured, they at least acknowledge that there is a clear difference between how we demonstrate and justify performance through the use of metrics and KPIs and how the outcome of library activity can be assessed.

Writing again in 2003, Poll suggests that the quality of a library service can be measured through the use of KPIs and the collection of statistics, by combining several statistical data regularly collected by libraries (Poll, 2003a, 2003b).

The potential problem with KPIs is that most library managers struggle to understand and identify the few management metrics which can be regarded as vital and subsequently worked into a KPI. Instead they try to collect and report on anything and everything that can be counted or measured and subsequently end up drowning in data! This is not a desirable situation, but often the experience of being 'statistic rich' and 'information poor' results in library managers choosing to neglect KPIs completely, which is the other extreme but can be very damaging to an organisation in the long term.

9.1.1 My Library Is Better Than Your Library: Bigger, Longer, Richer, Stronger

As previously mentioned, for many years libraries, from all sectors have counted and reported upon anything that is easy to do so, and over time certain aspects of library activity have become easier to measure (e.g. through automated systems, Web analytics, etc.) and can provide library managers with very thorough sets of data, from which they are expected to make decisions. This includes things such as number of books in the collection, number of periodical titles, number of periodical back issues, number of DVDs, number of audio CDs, linear metres of special collections and archives, number of items withdrawn, number of items added to stock, number of study spaces, number of staff, number of book issues, number of reservations, number of e-journal titles, number of e-book titles, number of e-journal downloads, number of e-book chapter downloads, number of study spaces, number of computers, number of visits to the library, number of enquiries, headcounts of users in the library, number of Twitter followers, number of Instagram followers, number of Facebook 'likes', etc. These types of statistics can prove very useful and can help to inform some aspects of service or collection, but by themselves they are not KPIs. They are simply measures of quantity which can often be used to demonstrate how 'big' or 'small' a library collection is or can be an indicator of how much resource the library has or how many times the items in the library are used. This information might be useful but it does not provide any meaningful indication of how the library is performing without being grounded with a much wider context.

Many libraries make use of such statistics and derive them against other statistics and in doing so are able to tell a bit more of the story of how their library is being used. For example, if a library knows how many potential users it could have and how many they know who visit and use the library they can calculate the percentage of the possible population who are active library users; if a library knows how many books are issued and how many users it has it can report on ratios of book issues per active reader; if a library knows how much its overall expenditure is and how many active users it has it is possible to report on spend per active user, or number of staff per user, or number of e-resource downloads per user, etc.

Such information can certainly be of use internally for justifying expenditure, general reporting, or presenting business cases to the parent organisation, but they are still simply sets of inventory and usage statistics. Similarly, these types of statistics can be used to compare one library with another or within a group of libraries. A good example of this is the SCONUL statistics which is an initiative operated across all university and national libraries in the United Kingdom, whereby a standard set of statistics is collected and collated annually and individual institutions are able to compare and benchmark with each other.

However, usage and volume statistics as such do not by themselves qualify as KPIs. This is quite simply because they do not indicate performance, but simply size, usage, and levels of resourcing. They might, for example, show you that your library has more books than another, or fewer opening hours, or more staff per student, or more Twitter followers. There is no indication through these statistics alone that the performance of the library or the quality of the library experience is any better than it is at another library!

9.1.2 Is a Service Standard a KPI?

Service standards (or customer service standards) are highly valuable as informative management tools, and in reporting back on them they do offer some insight into a library's performance, but like usage statistics, in themselves, they are not KPIs. The reason for this will become clear in the section to follow in which the characteristics of KPIs are unpicked. Service standards, by their nature should be outward facing and developed in order to manage customer expectation, which means they are set as aspirational targets. This means that they are unlikely to be indications of the handful of vital performance measures, which at a glance can tell you how the library is performing.

A quick Internet search for 'KPIs' or 'Key Performance Indicators' in academic libraries will result in a wealth of web pages where the library in question is proudly displaying their 'Key Performance Indicators' and is reporting back on their performance against them. This is very encouraging and is a wonderful customer service to be able to offer users and it really does enhance the user experience, but in almost all cases the KPIs on display are actually 'service standards' and are not characteristic if true KPIs. Examples of such service standards include:

- We will have 50% of returned books back on the shelf within one working day
- Our library search and discovery services will be available 97% of the time
- Our library web pages will be available 97% of the time
- 85% of print book orders will be received into the library within 4 weeks of the orders being placed
- We will have 80% of urgently requested books received in the library within 2 weeks of ordering
- The library will aim to be open 100% of advertised opening hours
- 90% of our PCs will be operational at any one time
- Interlibrary loans will be processed within one working day of receipt
- No user should wait to be acknowledged for more than 3 minutes to be helped by library front line staff
- All comments/feedback/suggestions from library users received via the online and printed comments scheme will receive a response within one working day
- We will achieve an average of over 90% satisfaction in our 'information skills' training sessions

Listing and reporting on such targets and standards is indeed good practice, but such reporting tends to be semesterly or annually, which means they cannot act as KPIs, as one of the characteristics of a KPI is that it needs to be frequently measured and reported on some that management decisions can be taken in order to change underperformance quickly.

Another KPI pitfall that many libraries seem to fall into is listing their targets against service area objectives and badging them as KPIs. Examples of these include:

Service Area/Objective	Target/Standard (NOT KPI)
To offer library inductions to new users	Achieve 55% take-up by new students
To provide a tailored service for disabled students	Contact students with disabilities within 3 working days of receiving declaration notification
To evaluate the effectiveness of information skills sessions	Achieve 70% satisfaction for information skills sessions
Provide skilled staff to support a quality library service	Conduct an annual audit of staff training needs and develop training plans
To engage with students to provide a responsive service	To attend a minimum of one Student/Staff Liaison committee per school per year annum

Again, displaying such information on the library web pages or in the libraries themselves this can be regarded as good practice for library services, but they differ from KPIs as they are measures against operational service objectives or service commitments. They are not indicators of current performance and should not be confused with KPIs which, if displayed to the library users (and they don't necessarily need to be) need to be associated to outcomes of service rather than objectives.

9.1.3 Common Misunderstandings – Summary

Before illustrating what makes a KPI and explaining the different characteristics of results and performance indicators the following table is presented to try to convey how some of the statistical measures described before can be presented as inventory statistics, usage statistics, and measurable standards. But without any other context none of these can be regarded as a KPI:

Statistics	Usage Statistic	Standard/Target
Number of books in collection	Number of books issued	To increase issue figures from previous year
	Percentage of active stock	50% of books are in circulation
Number of study spaces	Average occupancy of study spaces	To always have study spaces available
Number of bins	Number of bins with litter in them	To empty bins twice a day
Number of potential library users	Average daily visits to the library	To annually increase average daily visits

9.1.4 What Exactly Is a KPI Then?

Effective library managers understand the performance of all the key areas of their library and information service by distilling them down into critical KPIs. In order for KPIs to be the vital navigation tools to help you understand whether your library is on the 'right track' or not, we need to know what the 'right track' is. This is in fact the organisational or the library strategy and KPIs need to be closely linked to the outcomes that have been identified through the library's strategic planning.

> *Many organisations fall into the trap of retro-fitting objectives to existing and established metrics, which is simply back to front. KPI development has to start with your strategy and the objectives that the business is aiming to achieve*
> *(Marr, 2014, xiv)*

Performance frameworks, dashboards, or scorecards are used by many companies to group KPIs together to display 'at a glance' the overview of the business (or particular unit or department). The previous chapter focused on different methods and tools used for measuring performance in libraries and this included the use of the 'balanced scorecard', which has become a popular performance management tool for libraries. It is this use of the balanced scorecard which best lends itself to libraries developing and using meaningful performance indicators and KPIs as a fundamental part of its reporting.

KPIs therefore are often separated into the following key areas (i.e. those used in the balanced scorecard):

- Measurements of customer satisfaction
- Measurements of financial performance
- Measurements of internal processes
- Measurements of employee development and satisfaction

9.1.5 Measuring What Matters

As mentioned before, for KPIs to be meaningful to a library and information service they need to be closely related to strategy. Most library departments or units will have a strategic plan, or strategic direction, which in turn will be aligned with their parent organisation (e.g. university, school, NHS hospital trust, local council, etc.). With this in mind, it is important to remember that KPIs need to provide information and answers to what we need to know as library managers. We need to know what our information needs are and what we want answered before KPIs are developed in order to provide the answers. Asking broad 'performance questions' against your strategic headings can help to identify the metrics which will be able to demonstrate results or performance. For example, broad performance questions around customer satisfaction (an area of the balanced scorecard) might include: 'To what extent are we keeping customers that we have acquired?' or 'to what extent would our customers recommend our library to their friends?'

Another of the foremost commentators on KPIs, David Parmenter argues that "many companies are working with the wrong measures, many of which are incorrectly termed key performance indicators" (Parmenter, 2010, p. 1). He goes on to suggest that very few organisations, business leaders, writers, accountants, and consultants have fully explored what a KPI actually is, and the same might be said of libraries. In order to establish whether or not this is the case it is necessary to define Key Performance Indicators. According to Parmenter there are four different types of performance measure which need to be understood before a KPI can be used in the right context:

1. *Result Indicator (RIs)*	**2.** *Performance Indicators (PIs)*
RIs tell you what you have done	PIs tell you what to do
3. *Key Result Indicator (KRI)*	**4.** *Key performance Indicators (KPIs)*
KRIs tell you how you have done in a perspective or critical success factor	KPIs tell you what to do to increase performance dramatically

Many organisations, especially libraries, talk about KPIs without effectively demonstrating the difference between their results indicators and their performance indicators. Parmenter offers some examples of key results indicators, which are often mistaken for KPIs. These include customer satisfaction, profitability of customers, employee satisfaction, and return on capital employed (Parmenter, 2010, p. 2). The common characteristic of measures such as key results indicators (KRIs) is that they are achieved through the results of many different actions and present a clear picture as to the direction that the organisation is going in. KRIs typically cover a longer period of time than KPIs and are reviewed on a monthly, quarterly, or annual cycle, rather than on a weekly basis as KPIs should be.

KRIs within a library and information setting might therefore include customer satisfaction, employee satisfaction, return on investment in library services, etc.

KRIs provide information for those people working at board or governing body level, rather than those involved in the day-to-day management of the organisation. It is the KPIs which need to be monitored more frequently to ensure that the organisation is set to achieve the results it desires. Interesting libraries are usually a constituent part of a larger organisation (i.e. council, university, college, hospital, etc.) which means that those responsible for strategic leadership of the library service fall more into the 'management' category than the 'governing body' and therefore naturally inclined to pay attention to the detail of the library's KPIs.

In between KRIs and KPIs are numerous performance and results indicators. The balanced scorecard, as discussed in the previous chapter is an effective method for using and presenting top-level KRIs alongside significant KPIs and other performance and results indicators.

9.1.6 Now I'm Even More Confused!

Introducing results indicators and key performance questions can tend to overcomplicate the matter, but none the less, it is important for library managers to know of these tools so that their KPIs are genuine, meaningful, and can be used as KPIs are intended to be. Similarly, untangling KPIs from usage statistics and service standards can be equally as daunting. In brief KPIs are quantifiable measurements, agreed to in advance, that reflect the library's critical success. Library managers might have dozens of other statistics and metrics that let them know how things are running, but it is the few that you have developed as KPIs, which show how well the library is achieving against its strategic goals and objectives.

Very simply, KPIs are a high-level snapshot of an organisation based on specific, predefined measures.

9.1.7 KPI Best Practice Tips

- In order for an indicator to be regarded as 'key' it has to be related to the most important and critical aspects of your library service. The strategic objectives of the parent organisation should be what matters most and your KPI should link to this. KPIs need to help to monitor the execution of the strategy. Developing a strategy map which relates to the four balanced scorecard perspectives can help with placing your strategic objectives:
  - Objectives relating to customers and the market
  - Financial objectives
  - Internal business process objectives
  - Objectives relating to employees and organisational culture
- Always think about outcomes of your service. Senior managers are not interested in being bigger and better than somebody else's library. They need to be able to see how the library is having an impact and ultimately a positive outcome.
- Define the questions that you need to answer though your KPIs. KPIs have to be meaningful and relevant to your strategy.
- Every organisation (and every library) will probably have a different strategy and strategic objectives and drivers. In the same way every library will require a different set of KPIs. There will be some that are common across different libraries, but do remember that no two libraries are working to the same strategy. Be sure that your KPIs are fit for your library (not somebody else's).
- Make sure that your library's KPIs are owned by the right manager and that all staff understand why we are measuring something and why some things are 'key'. For every KPI introduced into the performance management framework, there must come with a rationale and understanding as to why this indicator is now all important and is a critical decision support tool. 'Buy in' is all important.
- Remember that KPIs are there to improve performance and lead to better decision making. If they do not do this then they do not need to be KPIs (i.e. they might be better placed elsewhere). It is important that the value of KPIs is not diminished by adding to the workload of collecting and analysing them. There is a danger, especially in libraries, for KPIs to be buried and lost within a large set of mediocre or less relevant metrics.

9.1.8 KPI Practices to Avoid

- *Measuring what other libraries measure.* In fact, don't measure things just because another library does. This is quite common in libraries and especially where there are sector benchmark groups, which encourage the collection and analysis if 'like' data sets. This can be useful for comparative evaluations, but remember that KPIs need to be subjective to your service, your institution, and your strategy.

- *Measuring things that are easy to collect or count.* Libraries often default to the metrics which are readily available in existing systems and procedures (i.e. the usage or inventory data). Invariably these won't be your KPIs. For many KPIs it is important to go beyond the face value of the numbers and analyse the meaning of the numbers.
- *Be wary of reporting on averages, percentages, and ratios.* That is not to say that such metrics may well be KPIs but a metric which has been calculated as 'average', or a 'percentage' is usually a storytelling statistic rather an indicator of performance against a given outcome.
- *KPIs need to be up to date and relevant for the operating year of your strategy.* It is important to regularly review your KPIs. You should be reporting on them regularly as well, so this should be obvious. It is less obvious when supposed KPIs are reported on an annual basis and become more 'historic' than useful.

In his book *Key Performance Indicators: Developing, Implementing and Using Winning KPIs* David Parmenter provides some excellent examples of Key Performance Indicators, which make it easy to see how simple KPIs can be. One of his examples, which does this is the example of an airline KPI:

This example concerns a senior British Airways official who set about turning British Airways around in the 1980s by reportedly concentrating on just one KPI. He was notified, wherever he was in the world, if a plane was delayed. The British Airways manager at the relevant airport knew that if a plane was delayed beyond a certain threshold, they would receive a personal call from this British Airways official. It was not long before British Airways planes had a reputation for leaving on time.

(Parmenter, 2010, p. 4)

Parmenter goes on to explain why this single KPI was so effective and how it affects all six of the Balanced Score card perspectives:

- *Financial* – Increased costs, including additional airport surcharges and the cost of accommodating passengers as a result of planes being curfewed
- *Customer* – Increased customer dissatisfaction and alienation of people meeting passengers at their destination (potential future customers)
- *Learning and growth* – Negative impact on staff development as they learned to replicate bad habits that created late planes
- *Internal processes* – Adversely affected supplier relationships and servicing schedules, resulting in poor service quality

- *Environment* – Contributed more to ozone depletion as additional fuel used in order to make up time on a flight
- *Employee satisfaction* – Increased employee dissatisfaction, as they were constantly firefighting and dealing with dissatisfied customers

This example shows how a KPI shows you what action needs to be taken to remedy the situation and in this instance runs deeply through the whole organisation that failing to meet the KPI can be tied to an individual team, which in turn means that all teams need to be focused in reaching that KPI, and ensuring that the plane leaves on time.

In another publication by Parmenter, he suggests that similar KPIs for government and no profit organisations (the category which libraries would fall into) include:

- *List of late projects, by manager, reported weekly, to the senior management team*
- *Number of initiatives implemented after, and as a result of, the staff satisfaction survey*
- *Number of confirmed volunteers for the annual street collection appeal*
- *Staff in vital positions who have handed in their notice on a given day*
- *Number of vacant managers registered for an in-house training event*

(Parmenter, 2012, p. 77)

Such KPIs are a useful pointer for libraries, but of course, these all focus on negative outcomes (if the KPI is not reached) and are designed to affect staff behaviours across the team to ensure that everyone is working for the same desired outcomes.

For library and information services KPIs can be applied in this way, but equally they can be used to positively indicate progress and success, and the following chapter about 'how KPIs can be used' will illustrate this.

CHAPTER TEN

How Can KPIs Be Used in Performance Measurement?

According to Holmes and Parsons (2016), some of the performance measures that we have looked at in this book, including external metrics and benchmarking, can help to inform internal planning and key performance indicators, which in turn is an effective and proactive way of ensuring a strategic approach to quality assurance and service development. He suggests that "[service] excellence is not necessarily achieved using traditional quality assurance processes but that it is more likely to be attained through strategic planning processes aligned with key performance indicators that provide accountability" (Holmes & Parsons, 2016, p. 25).

Having discussed the characteristics of both performance and results indictors, in the previous chapter, it is now useful to look at what libraries need to evaluate and how such indicators (including KPIs) might be applied within library and information performance measurement.

10.1 CAN VALUE AND IMPACT BE MEASURED THROUGH PERFORMANCE INDICATORS?

Using performance measurement to evidence the value and impact of a library or information service was discussed in Chapter 4 and we will make reference to this during this chapter. Libraries, across all sectors serve a particular purpose and set out to achieve goals and objectives as determined by the library's stakeholders. Such objectives will differ according to the nature and strategic function of the library and what the particular expectations of its user community are. If the library delivers its objectives effectively and achieves its aims or goals then there is a high likelihood that the library will have had an impact on the users and the communities which it serves, and through having an impact will be considered valuable, or to have value (either financial or otherwise) by those who use the library's services and facilities.

Libraries and Key Performance Indicators
http://dx.doi.org/10.1016/B978-0-08-100227-8.00010-8

One area of management to consider when discussing performance measurement is that of 'critical success factors' which are the areas in any business or organisation in which performance must be satisfactory (or above) in order that the organisation can perform well. In her book about the strategic management of information services, Corrall suggests that "critical success factors can be considered and investigated at various levels, but the most common approach is based on an aggregation of management perspectives, usually reached through structured discussions" (Corrall, 2000, pp. 104–105). In this, Corrall is suggesting that there is no right or wrong way to agree upon critical success factors and that, as high-level factors, they can be expressed in abstract terms. They then need to be systematically monitored and measured through the use of performance indicators. Examples of critical success factors for libraries might be having efficient and reliable suppliers; having motivated, skilled, and technically expert staff; having accessible service models; having a robust IT network infrastructure; being customer focused. Critical success factors can also be known as Key Results Areas or Key Performance Areas, both of which are defined in the previous chapter. Ultimately the success of these areas can be measured through performance indicators which should show, at a glance, what is being achieved. Corrall argues that library managers have traditionally found this difficult to achieve and have tended to 'measure the measurable' and concentrate on operational and financial data, which are effectively about 'inputs' (financial resources, staff resources, etc.) and 'outputs' (resources, catalogue records, study spaces, etc.) of the library. Hernon and Altman (2010) argue that library managers need to move their attention from inputs and outputs to outcomes and impacts. They regard input and output measures as 'outdated' and suggest that measures should specifically relate to customer-oriented outcomes and areas that need to improve. Essentially neither the quantity of library usage nor the quality of services offered and provided through libraries provide evidence of the impact that they have on their users, which is why we need to once again focus on the outcomes of library usage in order to start to discuss impact and value.

Many contemporary public library commentators, such as Brophy (2006) write enthusiastically and positively about public libraries and about libraries in general, often describing them as being at the centre of their society. Brophy suggests that "libraries are at the heart of social systems; they exist to serve the needs of people, to help them live, learn and develop and to act as part of the social glue which holds communities together"

(Brophy, 2006, p. 3). Therefore if this societal impact is to be truly demonstrated, then this can only be the case if public libraries are explicit about having 'social well-being' or 'social inclusion' outcomes.

The importance of having well-defined outcomes, and being able to measure the outcomes of libraries was briefly covered in Chapter 4, during the discussion about developing a culture of performance measurement. Linley and Usherwood argue that traditional input and output indicators for public libraries should be supplemented with qualitative data on outcomes related to library usage to reveal the social and economic impact and show their value extends beyond their established functions (such as education, leisure, culture, etc.). On this basis, public library success would be related to the social objectives and outcomes of their local authority (Linley & Usherwood, 1998).

10.1.1 Outcomes of Library Usage

It is appropriate to look a bit closer at what constitutes an outcome of using a library. Outcomes will differ depending upon the type of library under discussion and also on the mission of the individual library or library service.

The mission of most libraries is generally to provide and deliver information for the needs of a specified population. Other tasks such as legal deposit rights, preservation of rare materials, or special collections are, in most cases, subservient to the main purpose. Therefore the best testimony for a library's quality would be the influence of the library's products and services on the information literacy of its population.

(Poll, 2001, p. 709)

The concepts of an 'outcome' and the 'outcomes of library usage' have not changed. One particular definition, still applicable today is:

Outcomes can be seen as the eventual result of using library services, the influence the use had, and its significance to the user

(Revill, 1990, p. 316)

The earlier discussion focused on public libraries and their 'social missions', but equally academic libraries would invariably be supporting and delivering to educational and research missions, where the mission of a legal information service or law library might be to support its lawyers in achieving success in the courtroom. It should also be taken into account that the effects or results of using a library could be immediate or could only be realised later on in the longer term. They could be intended and planned for, or alternatively they could be unexpected.

Poll (2003a, 2003b) summarises the difference between short-term results of using libraries (perhaps even after a single visit) and longer term outcomes. For example, she suggests that short-term results include gaining information, solving problems, saving time (in study or professional work), improving information-seeking skills, or improving IT and computer skills. Longer term results and outcomes could include achieving information literacy, academic success, achieving employment or improving career prospects, changes in behaviour (Poll, 2003a, 2003b).

The influences and effects of library usage on users are complex and very difficult to evidence, especially if the actual outcome is not realised until sometime after the library usage (e.g. career progression) and the individuals or communities concerned might not attest their situation to previous library usage. To put this into context the following lists offer some suggested outcomes of different types of library usage:

Public libraries
- Social cohesion
- Community identity
- Economic regeneration
- Community well-being
- Literacy

Academic libraries
- Information literacy
- Student attainment / academic success
- Research impact

Health libraries
- Better informed/evidence-based practice
- Clinical competency levels
- Digitally literate patients

Any one of the previous outcomes (and these are only indicative) will have several layers of complexity within it and assessing them would not be without its difficulties. By way of illustration, if we take a single outcome, that of 'social cohesion' and think about what this looks like in the real world, it is plain to see that a great amount of work would need to done on any one particular outcome in order to effectively assess it. For example, in discussing the role of the public library in achieving social cohesion, some of the literature introduces the notion of the generation and exchange of social capital as being a positive outcome of library usage. There is now a general acceptance that public libraries contribute to 'community' and at least have the potential to have a very positive impact on civil society, which can be attributed to public libraries' contribution to the creation of social capital (Varheim, 2007). Through being both a central meeting space and a place from which public services are delivered, public libraries make a substantial contribution to the generation of social capital. This in turn is important in that 'communities high in social capital are characterised by citizenship, neighbourliness, trust and shared values, community involvement, volunteering, social networks and civic participation' (Goulding, 2004). If Goulding's findings are accurate for the whole sector, then the role of the public library in developing its users through social capital becomes all the more important in any mission to achieve social cohesion as an outcome. However, even measuring and demonstrating semitangible outputs such as the generation of social capital is difficult enough, let alone measuring outcomes such as social cohesion. This is one of the reasons why libraries (not just public) have traditionally tried to measure their impact and value through usage metrics and in particular 'value for money' type evidence, rather than trying to evidence outcomes.

Another example, illustrative of the complexities of assessing an outcome is that of 'information literacy', the achievement of which is often a desired outcome of higher education library use by students (although information literate users is most likely a desired outcome from any library service). As, all those working in information literacy will acknowledge this area is huge and articulating information literacy outcomes from library usage would require much more discussion than can be afforded on these pages. Suffice to say that information literacy outcomes can be subdivided into attributes such as students becoming aware of their information-seeking behaviours, students applying information-seeking skills to their research, students becoming independent learners and researchers.

Outcomes are essentially the positive results for users of libraries which are realised from their use of libraries (although outcomes can be negative as well as positive). There is plenty of evidence, as discussed before, to suggest that specific elements of library and information provision do have positive impact against intended outcomes and this is often presented through 'value and impact' studies.

10.1.2 Existing Value and Impact Studies

There is no shortage of evidence that the measurement of the value and the impact of libraries is a much discussed area. The opening chapters of this book along with the previous discussion about 'outcomes' of library usage illustrate this. The very fact that these themes are subject to so much discussion suggests that outcomes, and value and impact are very important factors when planning and managing library and information services.

Whilst a lot of this good practice in this area comes from the academic sector, one of the earliest examples comes from a paper reporting on two significant research projects which investigated the impact of library and information services in both the health sector and the finance sector. The two studies presented were based on impact and outcomes measures which tried to demonstrate the positive differences that access to the library and librarians made to important decisions. In the case of the health care sector this manifested itself in an impact on diagnosis, clinical decisions, and treatment, and for the financial sector case study, a change in decision-making behaviours of financial managers and executives (Marshall, 2007).

Libraries have always attempted to measure their performance in order to justify themselves and make business cases for resources and developments. As illustrated with the literature review so far, there is lots of discussion and debate about how libraries demonstrate and measure their value and impact, and how quite often measurements tend to focus on usage of libraries and resources and metrics around quantities (e.g. number of visits, number of loans, number of downloads). Being able to generate quantitative data about library usage also helps libraries to set key performance indicators, another tool by which libraries can measure their performance. Some of the best research in this area correlates library usage with tangible outcomes, for example the *Library Data Impact Project* demonstrates relationships between academic library usage and academic achievement (Stone, Pattern, & Ramsden, 2012).

An example of a more specific impact assessment within the academic library sector is that of the LIRG/SCONUL Impact Implementation Initiative, which looked to assess the impact of higher education libraries in the United Kingdom on learning, teaching, and research. The impact (or outcome) was seen in terms of whether the participating libraries had made a difference to its users as a result of a variety of a number of different interventions. The initiative then sought to develop methodologies to be used by libraries to measure their impact (Markless & Streatfield, 2005; Payne & Conyers, 2005). The outcomes of this particular initiative led to deeper understanding of how libraries support academic processes, improved dialogue with academics and stakeholders, library staff development, raised profile for the library.

Markless and Streatfield (2006) expand upon detail of the Impact Implementation Initiative, an action research programme to encourage systematic exploration of the issues and practices involved in gathering evidence of impact in university libraries. and report how, as a result of using their new impact assessment methodology, there is a much broader understanding, within the United Kingdom, of the impact that academic libraries have on the student or research experience, but not necessarily of academic achievement. These discussions continue to illustrate the complicated and varied nature of trying to measure a library's specific impact on an individual user or group of users. They invariably end up demonstrating a positive value on the library service, which assists in making financial and resource decisions, or in the case of Markless and Streatfield (2006), can effect positive changes in practice. However, even these examples of investment and commitment to value and impact assessment, on a national scale, do not really present the sector with a single methodology, or set of methodologies to do this, but rather a suite of techniques and recommendations as to how value and impact might be demonstrated. Similarly, the US-based 'Lib-Value' project, which was a series of seven projects aimed at developing a strategy and a collected method of tested methods and instruments to help libraries communicate the value of their services and operations (Mays, Tenopir, & Kaufman, 2010). That is not to say that this programme approach to investigating value and impact measures is wrong, it simply illustrates the vastness of the theme. For example, the highly acclaimed 'Lib-Value' project segments its research projects very widely and includes projects aimed at identifying the value of e-books, the use and impact of learning commons spaces, environmental impact of libraries, the impact of information skills teaching, and return on investment of academic libraries.

10.1.3 Financial Value of Libraries

One of the main US commentators on academic library value and impact and a driving force behind the LibValue programme is Carol Tenopir. She has done much work on the 'return on investment' of academic libraries and suggests that return on investment allows a library to quantify and demonstrate the library's economic value to the institution.

> *For every euro or dollar or yen spent on the library, the university receives euros or dollars or yen back in the form of additional grants, income or donations, or long term value to the community from an educated workforce, more productive faculty and more successful students*
>
> *(Tenopir, 2010, p. 40)*

The main focus of the LibValue programme is to illustrate return on investment and a progress report suggests that the strands of the programme are producing such outcomes, although in some instances, such as the strand looking at the 'Value of library instructional services to teaching and learning' demonstrate a lot of what the project calls 'implied value', in that respondents tend to acknowledge the benefit of using library resources in terms of 'time saved' and also report 'improvement in their students work as a result of using library resources' (Tenopir & Fleming-May, 2011).

It is evident from the literature that during the period from 2005 to 2010, being able to demonstrate return on investment in library resources, particularly with regard to its impact on research, was becoming increasingly important. This extended not just to the major US academic research libraries, but further field to Europe and also to the publishers and aggregators of electronic library resources (Luther, 2008). An insightful case study to come from this period is that of the University of Illinois at Urbana-Champaign and a piece of research into return on investment which they undertook with the publisher Elsevier. Again, Tenopir is involved with this case study as it was clearly linked to (although not part of) the LibValue programme. The objective of the research was to be able to demonstrate that investment into digital and electronic library resources generates higher usage and ultimately higher quality research output. Being able to demonstrate such an impact is clearly a significant instrument when libraries come to set business cases for funding. Luther, herself a consultant to Elsevier, discusses how the case study which effectively demonstrates a return on investment paves the way for academic libraries to negotiate with their own institutions. Of course, being able to demonstrate that library usage has such a positive outcome and a positive impact on research and scholarship, and therefore the potential for the institution to bring in even more funding from an increase in research grants, is to be celebrated. The unfortunate factor about using return on investment to demonstrate value, and particularly when it is pushed and promoted by commercial publishers, is that it seems to be almost entirely driven by economics, rather than impact and value on society for the greater good.

Tenopir however argues for libraries being able to demonstrate 'actual value' as well as 'implied value'. Libraries need to be clear about the exchange value of what they provide (i.e. the amount that one is willing to pay for information and access to it) and the use value of that information (i.e. the outcome or favourable result of using that information). Her case study, at the University of Illinois involved the qualitative analysis of how researchers perceived the benefit and value of the library, in use value, and provided a method for translating this into a quantitative measure with regard to how much exchange value was generated as a result of financial investment in the library.

10.2 USING INDICATORS TO MEASURE VALUE

Invariably providing evidence of value for money will require statistical data. This might be a financial return or a return on investment type ratio. The metrics and usage data which library and information services habitually collect allow for this evidence and by periodically checking usage figures (e.g. gate-counts, downloads, spend on resources) library and information managers are engaging and using results indicators and performance indicators. Derived indicators can also be used for the same purpose (e.g. number of books per library user).

In Chapter 9 we looked at the difference between results indicators and performance indicators and between key results indicators and key performance indicators. Where an overall Return on investment in a given period should be regarded as a Key Result Indicator, there are several performance indicators which sit beneath it (remember, Key Results are the result of many actions). For example:

Key Result Indicator (Value)	Performance Indicator
Return on investment into the library service	• Number of downloads per registered library user • Number of loans per registered library user • Number of downloads per e-journal title • Number of downloads per e-book • Number of library users receiving information skills training per librarian • Number of enquiries received • % of stock borrowed • Cost per download • Cost of book stock per registered library user • Cost of book stock per potential library user (i.e. wider community) • % increase in book loans • % increase in downloads • % increase in number of library users receiving information skills training • % increase of enquiries dealt with

Customer satisfaction with the library service (%)	• Number of complaints • % decrease in customer complaints • % increase in positive comments received • Average time taken to receive a reservation • Average time taken to receive an interlibrary loan • % decrease in time taken to receive a reservation • % decrease in time taken to receive an interlibrary loan • Number of study places available per user • % increase of study spaces available per user

10.3 USING INDICATORS TO MEASURE PERFORMANCE AGAINST OUTCOMES

As illustrated in the opening chapters, statistical data about the quantity of usage can show, to some extent, how much a library's services and resources has been drawn upon but for many library and information services there is a perception that high usage indicates that the service is beneficial to its users. However, "usage is not synonymous with value" (Troll, 2001). Roswitha Poll (2003a, 2003b) clearly demonstrates that key performance indicators take the collection of statistics a step further by combining several statistical data in order to demonstrate the quality of a library service but not necessarily the benefits of using a service. She goes on to discuss measuring the 'outcome' of a library and being able to assess the different aspects of 'outcome' and demonstrate the benefits that a library has on its users. However, there is no internationally agreed or tested method for assessing the different aspects of library 'outcomes'.

Having positive outcomes and being able to demonstrate them means that the library and information manager needs to be able to measure them and as has already been established, measuring outcomes is not about quantity nor quality and therefore poses quite a challenge.

A library outcome (e.g. an information literate community, delivery of world class research, social, cohesion, etc.) should be regarded as Key Results. A Key Results Indicator should give a clear picture as to whether the library is achieving this result and travelling in the right direction. As, Key Results Indicators are the results of many actions and activities, there is a sublevel behind each KRI which can be measured through performance indicators. For example:

Key Result Indicator (Outcome)	Performance Indicators
% of community regarded as information literate	• % of library users confident in searching for and retrieving information resources • % increase of library users confident in searching for and retrieving information resources • % of library users confident in navigating electronic library resources • % increase of library users confident in navigating electronic library resources • Decrease in number of enquiries compared against increase in use of e-resources
% of community regarded as socially engaged	• % of community (potential library users) attending reading groups • % increase of community (potential library users) attending reading groups • % increase in loans of dual language resources • Increase in requests for dual language resources • Number of outreach activities delivered • Number of new library memberships resulting from outreach activities
% of institution's research outputs regarded as 'world class'	• % increase of articles and research papers submitted to institutional repository • Number of citations of items contained within institutional repository • % increase in number of citations of items contained within institutional repository

The characteristics of a performance indicator (PI) are that, while important, they are not critical to delivering the intended results, but help to align the activity of the service with the library's overall strategy (in this case achievement of its outcomes). Key performance Indicators, on the other hand, are a set of these measures which are the most critical (critical success factors) for achieving successful outcomes. Characteristics of KPIS are as follows:

• They are nonfinancial measures
• They are measured frequently (e.g. daily, weekly)
• They would be acted upon by the head of the library service
• They clearly indicate what action needs to be taken to remedy the situation if negative or adverse performance is indicated
• They have a significant impact on achieving outcomes and results
• They tie responsibility down to a team

A KPI will have some or all of these characteristics. It is difficult to list a set of definitive KPIs as they would be relative to the desired outcomes, and strategic drive of an individual library or organisation. Suffice to say they would not be dissimilar to some of the performance indicators already listed, but the context and strategic priority of the respective library and information service would need to be taken into account. The following chapter will provide some of this context as it looks at five different case studies and how Key performance Indicators can be applied in different library and information environments.

CHAPTER ELEVEN

Case Studies

Elizabeth Malone, Head of Content Development, Co-director –
Library and Learning Services, Kingston University, London, United
Kingdom.

11.1.1 Aligning KPIs – KPIs in Action at Kingston University

Our journey in exploring and implementing Key Performance Indicators
(KPIs) at Kingston University has embraced four stages:

- Responding to university-level KPIs
- Developing departmental KPIs
- Exploring Service Standards
- Using data to drive continuous service improvement

The journey began back in 2012 with the launch of a new strategic plan for
the University – *Led by Learning* (Kingston University, 2012). This was
underpinned by three core strategies for Education, Research, and Enter-
prise, along with a number of supporting strategies including Information,
Finance, Estates, and People. Within these strategies were embedded a range
of KPIs and as part of the annual planning cycle, each department was asked
how they would respond to these. Not an unreasonable request but a challenging one when, to the layperson's view, some of the KPIs were
completely unintelligible! I suspect few of us in the library environment
are totally familiar with the intricacies of the Gearing Ratio or our university's external borrowings as a multiple of EBITDA! Fortunately for us, buried in the depths of the Education Strategy were KPIs we could identify
with, most notably:

% of students taught at Kingston University expressing overall satisfaction
with their course. Current 79%, improvement towards 83%, exceeding sector median by 2015/16.

Libraries and Key Performance Indicators
http://dx.doi.org/10.1016/B978-0-08-100227-8.00011-X

With university reputations rising and falling on the basis of the National Student Survey (NSS)[1] and with the library being able to identify directly with what was then Question 16 of the survey, this was clearly an area where our own desire to improve would directly contribute to the university's performance. We therefore rephrased the KPI to refer specifically to the library:

> % of students taught at Kingston University expressing overall satisfaction with the library. Current 78% (benchmark 81%), to be within 1% of the sector average or greater by 2016.

Of course having a strategically aligned KPI does not magically achieve performance improvement! The next stage of our journey was to revisit the statistical data we collected, to analyse why we collected it, and to evaluate whether it contributed to measuring our performance and impact; and of course to decide whether we were collecting the right data. We did this through discussions within our departmental management team and team briefings, some real research using our own e-resources, the occasional Google search and, being librarians, asking others. From this we developed our own set of KPIs which we then embedded into our annual Operational Plan. The KPIs touched on most areas of library activity and we recognised that some would be more challenging to measure than others. For example, Information Expenditure per Full Time Equivalent student is a standard measure provided by the SCONUL Statistical Return.[2] However, measuring that an information literacy session had been offered to all campus–based students in level 4 and at dissertation level was more difficult to pin down and impossible to benchmark. We agreed to review our KPIs during our departmental management meetings and to report back on them as part of the planning round follow-up. Despite having set us the challenge in the first place, rather frustratingly the Planning Office did not request the data the following year – so we decided to supply it anyway!

[1] HEFCE, National Student Survey results http://www.hefce.ac.uk/lt/nss/results/2016 (Accessed 31 January 2017).

[2] SCONUL, Annual Statistics https://www.sconul.ac.uk/page/sconul-statistics-reports (Accessed 31 January 2017).

A year after setting our initial KPIs, departmental restructuring presented us with some new opportunities for reviewing our performance and stretching our goals for delivering an improved student experience. De-convergence from IT left us as a new department with a blank sheet of paper with regard to our objectives, our mission, vision, and values. It also cemented our decision to embrace a tool that we believed would enable us to achieve the KPIs we had set – Customer Service Excellence. This award, which is backed by the UK government, places KPIs and Service Standards as a key component of delivering and measuring good customer service. A departmental-wide training event enabled all our staff to discuss the kind of department we wanted to be. Feedback from this event was collated in the form of a word cloud and those words were then identified in the university's *Led by Learning* strategy and went on to form our values – the seven 'Cs' of:

- Customer Service
- Commitment
- Communication
- Community focus
- Creativity
- Collaboration
- Change

Our updated annual Operational Plan outlined where these featured in our objectives and staff were then asked during appraisal to link their own objectives to these values.

With Customer Service Excellence in mind, we identified a range of Service Standards which complemented our existing KPIs. Many of the standards were things we were already doing but they had never been written down, publicised to staff or students, or measured in a robust manner. Customer Service Excellence instilled a new rigour to our data collection and also produced the odd surprise. Our staff were supremely confident in setting a standard that declared all returned stock would be readily available in a public area in classmark order within 24 hours or one working day of return – except that it wasn't! Or at least it was for most of the year when our Night Team moved trolleys on a regular basis and our LRC Assistants were shelving during the evening. As soon as examinations finished and the library went quiet, trolleys were not moved at the same rate and our quarterly spot check for this standard revealed that the service fell considerably below our expectation. It was a very simple improvement to make to ensure trolleys were moved and emptied once a day, even if they weren't full! It is also a very simple demonstration of how measurement and targets can drive service improvement.

Both of KPIs and Service Standards are now reviewed regularly by the library management team but we have also convened a Value and Impact Strategy Group to lead our work in this area. Part of the role of this group is to champion the use of our data through publications such as our Annual Review and digital signage where we have been able to use infographics to summarise our achievements.

STUDENT SATISFACTION

Student Satisfaction with Library Services - Measured by the NATIONAL STUDENT SURVEY	Intended direction	Value 2013/14	Value 2014/15	Value 2015/16	Value 2016/17
To be within 1% of sector average or greater by 2016 — Sector average in 2016 = **88%**	⬆	82%	85%	87%	88%

Student Satisfaction with LRCs - Measured by the LRC USER SURVEY	Intended direction	Value 2013/14	Value 2014/15	Value 2015/16	Target achieved
Overall, the LRCs provide a good service	⬌	87%	89%	95%	✔
I am satisfied with the quality of customer service	⬌	90%	95%	95%	✔
I am satisfied with the library support for my academic needs	⬆	85%	88%	89%	✔

The group is also looking at how to push our use of performance data even further. As part of our analysis of the free text comments in the NSS and our LRC User Survey, we are looking for emerging themes that could potentially be addressed through either a KPI or Service Standard. We are also considering how to use complementary data generated by other techniques such as a recent ethnographic study carried out in partnership with our students and the use of tools such as Touchstone Tours.

Which leaves us with the question of whether we have achieved what we set out to do? Our primary goal was to improve the experience of our students in using the library services at Kingston University and to see that realised through improvement in the National Student Survey results. In this respect we have moved to where we wanted to be. Our score in both 2015 and 2016 equalled the national benchmark. Our challenge now is to exceed that.

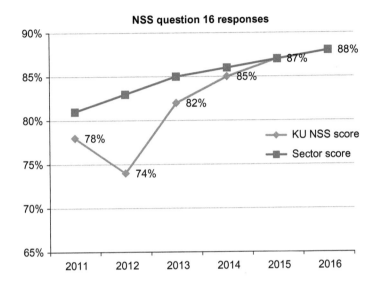

11.2 LIVERPOOL JOHN MOORES UNIVERSITY

Elaine Sykes, Team Leader (Business Control), Library Services, Liverpool John Moores University, Liverpool, United Kingdom.

11.2.1 Using KPIs to Evaluate Strategy

11.2.1.1 Background

This case study presents the experience encountered at Liverpool John Moores University (LJMU) in using KPIs to assess the success of its strategic plan. LJMU is a post-92 institution with a strong teaching focus, based in the North West of England. Its three libraries currently serve approximately 25,000 students.

In 2014 Library Services, LJMU was due to create its new strategic plan. This was a time of change for the department, as it was coming out of a period of disaggregation from the former converged service (with Student Services), and re-establishing itself as a more traditional library service again. In addition, a new director had recently started. As a result, the new strategy was a timely opportunity to reconsider its purpose and vision, in light of its recent changes.

The strategy was written as a result of two Management Team Away Days, attended by all library managers, representing all areas of the service. There, a decision was taken for the Library Services Strategic Plan to reflect the wider University strategy, and it was therefore split into four main strands: Establishing and Enhancing the Student Partnership, Excellence in Learning, Teaching and Assessment, Embedding Research and Scholarship and Social and Economic Engagement.

It was also felt that there was a need to establish a framework by which to be able to measure the success of these strategic aims. The method chosen for this was to establish appropriate KPIs for each aim of the strategic plan. A subgroup of Management Team was formed to consider this further.

11.2.1.2 Establishing the Framework

Led by the Associate Director, the subgroup set about identifying appropriate KPIs for each area of the strategy document. This was done through lengthy discussions, but it was soon found that for each of the strategic aims, the following two questions proved extremely helpful;

1. How would this strategic aim manifest itself in day-to-day operations?

2. What data could demonstrate that this is occurring?

For example, under the theme of 'Excellence in Learning, Teaching and Assessment', there was a strategic aim to enhance digital and information skills. Considering the previous two questions, it was apparent that operationally this would mean the Academic Liaison Librarians providing sessions that delivered relevant skills in an engaging way. To answer the second question, the answer was via surveys taken at the end of each skills session delivered, asking participants to give the session a rating.

For some strategic aims, the KPIs seemed rather natural – the relevant data was available and followed logically from existing operations. Other areas were more difficult. In particular this was around the newer areas of library activity, such as research, where the possible data available was unknown at the start of the strategic period.

In addition, it was difficult to express the data in such a way that it would be a meaningful KPI and not just a service metric. This meant changing thinking to take into account relative measures, rather than absolute. For example, considering percentage increases rather than totals in activity levels.

One key point is that the subgroup were keen to not just include front facing data but also to cover wider business activities of the department. As a result, five KPIs were included which measured staff training and development, such as the percentage of staff who had attended training sessions in the period.

11.2.1.3 Summary of KPIs

The subgroup came up with a list of 46 recommended KPIs, which, as a whole, could be taken as a way to measure the effectiveness of the agreed strategy and, after a small period of negotiation, were approved by senior library managers. As a result, they were explicitly incorporated into the strategy narrative document which was produced.

In actuality, this approach was very timely for two reasons. Firstly, it coincided with the department's application for a Customer Service Excellence kitemark. As part of this exercise, the department developed a comprehensive set of 44 service standards, including challenging targets. There was a good deal of crossover between these and the strategic KPIs and each set has helped uphold the other.

Secondly, the department was required to start submitting monthly performance indicator reports to the University's Senior Management Team. Again, this dovetailed nicely with this work on KPIs and helped establish regular performance measurement into the library culture.

11.2.1.4 Successes

One of the main successes of this approach to strategy was in providing a rationale and a framework by which to regularly report, check, and analyse library data. This was the first time that the department had attempted this approach and therefore, although it was a steep learning curve, it did implement several positive changes within the department. Some particular successes were as follows:

Library standards – Driven by both the need to measure strategy, and also achieve Customer Service Excellence kitemark, the establishment of the existing library standards has been a real highlight of the last strategic period. Their comprehensiveness and challenging targets have inspired a more consistent service, with customers aware of what they can expect from the service.

Staff engagement – As a result of this work, staff are generally accepting of using performance indicators to measure success. It has been clear from the start that this is not about measuring individual performance levels, or allocating blame, but merely to highlight areas for development.

Another contributing factor to achieving good staff engagement was the inclusion of wider KPIs than just those relating to front facing services. This meant that all staff felt like they had a contribution to make in successfully delivering the strategy.

Setting priorities – Having more reliable, richer, regular data means that managers are more likely to consult and trust the information provided. As a result, there has been greater data-driven decision making. In turn, it is anticipated that having a more solid data foundation will give a useful baseline with which to compare new initiatives in order to demonstrate value and impact.

11.2.1.5 Issues Encountered

We were unable to fully realise all the statistics that we had intended at the beginning of the strategic process. This was due to a number of factors including:

Availability of data – for some of the KPIs, data was either impossible to collect or extremely limited. Some data relied on the ability to carry out unlimited surveys, which was hindered by university restrictions. Some relied on systems becoming more discerning than proved to be the case, and some could only be measured by relatively simplistic mechanisms (e.g. paper tracking slips).

Data quality – Where data was available, there were still some quality issues. For example, some of the manually input data (e.g. headcounts) would contain errors or missing entries which therefore required significant data cleaning before it could be used. Similarly, there were some issues experienced in terms of classifying different types of study spaces which made establishing relative measures difficult.

Emergent events – As with most strategies, it is impossible at the start to predict all of the events which will take place over the coming years. As a result, emergent events overtook developments in other areas. For example, at the time of composition, the library had established a 'Critical Friends' group which acted as a small focus group, positive engagement with which was included as a Strategic KPI. Over time, and due to a lack of student engagement with this forum, the format was changed to create a deliberately informal casual 'drop in' environment.

In order to respond to such events, it would be useful to review the KPI set annually, in order to ensure that it continues to be fit for purpose and can adapt to emerging events.

Appropriate staff resource – This level of data gathering and analysis requires significant staff time and resource. Data analysis is still a fledgling area within academic libraries (albeit growing), and therefore it is not a common skill. This meant a large amount of work fell upon a small number of individuals, and it was not possible to establish all KPI measures.

11.2.1.6 Other Limitations

Measuring quantity, not quality – In common with many library service measures, these KPIs mainly focussed on transactional encounters, such as percentage of enquiries answered at the first point of contact. Although useful in themselves, there was a real focus on those measures for which data was available, rather than those which were most appropriate or that would offer most insight.

Too much emphasis on the quantitative – KPIs are by definition quantitative in nature. However, when it comes to examining quality in a library context, qualitative measures are invaluable in delivering insight and richer data. This is particularly true of those areas of service which are not merely transactional in nature, but meet a deeper, less tangible need, such as information skills.

Too internally focussed – The KPI set agreed on was extremely insular in its approach. As a result, its only frame of reference was historic performance. However, the SCONUL and NSS data sets provide a rich source of data with which to benchmark how LJMU performance compares to comparator institutions. Events showed that external benchmarking was a valuable source of information on performance, and therefore, this should be included in future KPI sets.

11.2.1.7 Lessons Learned

As a result of this experience, the following lessons were learned:

- Set KPIs at the same time as the strategy so they complement each other
- Consider the operational impact of the proposed strategy and use this as a basis for setting appropriate KPIs
- KPIs must be specific, and include challenging, but achievable, targets

- Evaluate the KPI set at least annually to ensure that it aligns with any emergent strategy that has developed in the year
- Be selective with KPIs – a lot of library data is available, but that doesn't mean it is all necessary
- Ensure KPIs cover all service activity, including nonfront facing services
- Include external measures, using external data to benchmark against comparator institutions
- Make use of as much automated data as possible
- Have a complementary qualitative data framework to ensure that stakeholders are engaging as expected by the strategy
- Allocate sufficient and appropriate resource

11.2.1.8 Going Forward

This approach has been mostly successful, particularly in two areas. Firstly, it has helped the department develop more of a culture of KPIs internally and the need to use quantitative measures to evidence performance. This has been a slow but steady change in service management, and there is a greater willingness and engagement to use quantitative evidence as a basis for decision making, and evaluation.

Secondly, it has established a sound baseline from which to build further. As mentioned before, the existing data sources currently have many limitations. However, as a result of this work, the department is working on a collaborative project with its IT Services department concerning using business intelligence software to interrogate an internal data warehouse. This has meant that less staff time is required for data entry and cleaning, and more time can be spent on analysis and developing insight. In addition, the data warehouse is able to provide richer, more joined-up data on customers, and enables the department to build greater customer profiles.

With regards to the next departmental strategic plan, it is highly likely that this KPI approach to measurement will be employed again in some way in order to measure its effectiveness. However, with the benefit of 3 years' experience in using data, there is greater scope to include more meaningful quantitative measures and also find a way to incorporate qualitative data to create a more rounded indicator of success.

11.3 MCMASTER UNIVERSITY

Kathryn Ball, Director, Assessment & Accountability, McMaster University Library, Hamilton, ON, Canada

11.3.1 Background

McMaster University is a medium-sized, medical doctoral university located in Hamilton, Ontario, Canada with a student population of 28,000 FTE. McMaster University Libraries comprise four physical locations: Mills Memorial Library, H.G. Thode Library of Science & Engineering, Innis (Business) Library, and the Health Sciences Library with over two million titles held, 130 staff, and a total operating budget of $22 million (CAN) for the reporting year 2014–15.[3] The Health Sciences Library is administered separately.

In 2009 McMaster University Library, excluding the Health Sciences Library, participated in a pilot project offered by the Association of Research Libraries (ARL) that provided the library with the opportunity to develop a new strategic plan using the Balanced Scorecard framework. Like many academic libraries, McMaster struggled to manage a large number of strategic objectives (over 60 at one point). The Library also collected large amounts of data but did not consistently link this data to the strategic plan. It was hoped that participation in this ARL initiative would result in a more effective planning process. Three other academic libraries participated in the project's first cohort: the Sheridan Libraries, Johns Hopkins University; University of Virginia Library; and the University Libraries, University of Washington (Kyrillidou, 2010).

The Balanced Scorecard is a strategic planning model and performance management tool developed by Robert Kaplan and David Norton that "translates an organization's mission and strategy into a comprehensive set of performance measures that provides the framework for a strategic measurement and management system" (Kaplan & Norton, 1986, p. 2). The process begins with identifying high-level strategic directions or objectives (referred to as the 'Strategy Map' in the Balanced Scorecard terminology) and then determining key performance indicators (known as measures), with specific targets, that will gauge the organisation's success in achieving its goals. The final step is putting in place strategic initiatives or projects that align with the strategic directions and that will help to ensure that the targets are met. The 'balance' in the system is the result of the four different perspectives that make up the framework: financial, learning and growth, internal processes, and customer, each with its own set of objectives, measures, and initiatives.

---

[3] CARL Statistics 2014–15 http://www.carl-abrc.ca/wp-content/uploads/2016/10/CARL-ABRC_Stats_Pub_2014-15.pdf.

In addition to Kaplan and Norton's classic work, the Library found Matthews' book on developing a scorecard for libraries to be a useful reference (Matthews, 2008).

In McMaster University Library's experience with the Balanced Score-card process, the development of a solid set of measures has proven to be the most challenging and time-consuming part of the implementation. Starting with a freshly crafted set of strategic directions, 13 in total, the Library needed between 2 and 4 measures for each direction. The scorecard imple-mentation team, made up of an Associate University Librarian, the Director of Assessment, and a librarian from the Collections division, decided to assign the task to groups of staff with a direct interest in a particular strategic direction. The working groups were charged with coming up with four to six possible measures, with the assistance of a member of the scorecard implementation team.

The working groups were reminded of the characteristics of a good mea-sure: specific, measurable, attainable, relevant, time based, or SMART. As a starting point they were asked to consider 'How would you know you were successful?' in achieving the specific strategic objective. They were also encouraged to consider data that the Library was already collecting, e.g. annual statistical surveys, regular user surveys such as LibQUAL[4] in order to minimise the number of new data sets to be collected. The final directive was that their recommended measures should have different time periods in order to avoid having a suite of 'annual' measures.

Once they had some ideas for possible measures many groups found it helpful to complete the standardised measures template created by the imple-mentation team. The simple form required the teams to assign their measure a meaningful name, to describe it in simple terms, to document the source of the data, the formula they would use for generating the number, how often the measurement would be gathered, and who would be responsible for doing this work. In order to ensure that the measure truly was 'measurable', the working group members were also asked to consider what the chart or table would look like? What number would the Library be scoring on? The task was challenging for the groups and a frequent comment from members was the concern that two or three measures could not capture all possible aspects of an objective. The members of the implementation team frequently reminded the groups that the Library was looking for measures

---

[4] LibQUAL https://www.libqual.org/home.

of 'strategy' and not 'operational' measures; that the measures were meant to serve as indicators of the progress that the Library was making to achieve its goals. It also became apparent that the implementation team would have to resist the search for the perfect measure and that the working groups would have to be content with measures that were 'good enough', at least at this point in the process.

The working groups generated a list of more than 60 measures that were vetted by the scorecard implementation team and reduced to a final list of 25 measures. This list was shared with all library staff for comment before being approved by the Library's senior management team. The final list was also shared with Deans, key campus partners, and other senior leaders at the university level. Although this process was very time consuming (several months elapsed from the time the working groups were set up to the final slate of measures) it proved to be very worthwhile both in terms of the quality of the resulting measures but also in terms of staff engagement in the process.

The final slate of measures for the Library's first scorecard was a mix of data the organisation was already collecting (e.g. gate count) and data it hoped to gather (e.g. average time to resolve IT problem reports); responses to specific questions on surveys that were regularly offered (e.g. LibQUAL[4]) and on surveys yet to be developed. For some of the measures, no targets were identified because the Library was collecting the information for the first time, and it was decided to hold off on establishing a benchmark until sufficient data had been reviewed to establish a realistic target. The effectiveness of the measures only became apparent once the scorecard implementation team began collecting the data and preparing it for presentation to the Library's senior management team.

In McMaster Library's implementation of the Balanced Scorecard, the measures data were part of the content of a monthly (i.e. September to April) strategy meeting with senior management. Each month focused on one perspective of the scorecard, e.g. the customer (or in McMaster's nomenclature, user) perspective. A member of the scorecard implementation team gathered the data from the appropriate data providers for all of the measures for that perspective and prepared one or two page reports for each measure using a common format in Excel that included the objective, measure, formula, target, score, data tables, data charts, notes, comments, and recommendations. In addition, they would also request brief progress reports from the leads of the strategic initiatives or projects that aligned with the measures under review. All documents were sent out in advance so that everyone was prepared for the discussion. Once 'approved' by senior management, the measures data sheets and the progress reports for the strategic initiatives were posted to the Library's website as part of the effort to make the strategic planning process more transparent to staff and users.

The goal of the strategy meetings was to focus discussion on the progress the Library was making on achieving its strategic directions. However, in the first year a substantial amount of time was spent on discussing and refining the measures. In some cases, it was a matter of setting or adjusting the target. In the Balanced Scorecard, the target should be aspirational and represent a stretch for the organisation. If the target was easily met, and it was expected that the Library would continue to meet the target, it was adjusted upwards. In other cases the opposite was true and the target was adjusted downwards. For some measures it became apparent that although the formula seemed plausible when crafted, when it came time to prepare the data for the management meeting the scorecard implementation team was no longer convinced of the measure's clarity. This was often the case with 'omnibus' measures that had been crafted to pool the results from several disparate data elements (e.g. multiple categories of instruction activities or library promotion activities). It was often decided to simplify the measure by pulling it apart, scoring on the one most strategic element, and including the other data as additional information. There were other measures that, while admittedly unsophisticated or incomplete, were adopted as reasonable until a better measure was found. For example, the Library would have preferred an 'outcome' or 'impact' measure for its instructional services, but agreed to use the number of instruction sessions and number of participants as a reasonable first step. Some measures entailed a significant amount of work to collect the data such as developing an in-house survey to determine service or collection satisfaction. In all cases, that did not happen in the first year of the Balanced Scorecard, even with the best of intentions.

After having reviewed all of the measures twice during the first year it became clearer to the scorecard implementation team which measures were working and which were not. Of the 25 measures on the scorecard 18 were 'active', with current data. Although the scorecard implementation team tweaked some measures it tried to resist adding additional measures and making dramatic changes to the original slate. It was important for the Library to have a set of measures that would last the life of its strategic plan, i.e. 5 years for comparative purposes.

In addition to serving as indicators of the Library's success in achieving its strategic directions, the measures have provided useful data for decision making in recent years. As a result of regular tracking and reviewing the data from specific measures, the Library decided to redesign its fund-raising web pages, to hire a part-time public relations manager, and to add more silent and quiet study seats in its science and engineering library.

With the expiration of the existing strategic plan in 2014, the Library conducted a new strategic planning exercise that resulted in an updated plan to see the Library through to 2020. The Library, recognising the value in the Balanced Scorecard with its holistic approach and strategic alignment of directions and metrics, was committed to using the framework once again, with one minor adjustment. It was decided to replace one of the perspectives, internal processes, with community engagement which had become a priority for both the Library and McMaster University in recent years.

With a new set of strategic directions it was important to refresh the scorecard and to develop a new slate of metrics. The process was much more streamlined the second time around and there was a desire to move ahead with a lean, crisply defined set of measures drawing on data that was either readily available or reasonably attainable by the organisation. The scorecard team had been replaced by the Strategic Planning Committee, composed of representatives from the three staff groups (librarians, managers, library assistants), the University Librarian (ex officio), and chaired by the Director of Assessment, who assumed responsibility for both the scorecard and general oversight of the organisation's strategic planning process. This committee reviewed the previous slate of measures, recommending those that could be carried forward for use in the new scorecard because of the strong linkages to the new strategic directions. New measures were shared with the library staff for feedback and ultimately finalised by the senior management team.

McMaster Library's current set of measures is available on its website at http://library.mcmaster.ca/library-scorecard. The Library's senior management team continues to hold monthly strategy meetings with the Director of Assessment sharing measures' data and updates from the strategic projects from each of the four perspectives. The scorecard, and its metrics, continue to be the framework for the Library's strategic conversations and decision making.

11.4 PRINCIPLES FOR BETTER METRICS – AN APPROACH IN NHS LIBRARY AND KNOWLEDGE SERVICES

Alan Fricker & Tracey Pratchett

11.4.1 Introduction

Library and Knowledge Services (LKS) for the NHS in England are currently embarking on a transformational programme of development. The Knowledge for Health care Framework (KfH) has a broad and ambitious scope tackling multiple aspects of the services to be provided over a 5-year period to 2020 (Health Education England, 2014). Sponsored by Health Education England this programme will profoundly affect LKS across England positioning them to maximise their impact and thrive (Fig. 11.1).

Fig. 11.1 Knowledge for Health care work streams. *(Reproduced with the permission of Health Education England.)*

A small number of metrics for success were identified as part of the initial framework document – for example 'Double the amount of investment in national, collaborative procurement of e-resources'. The difficulties experienced by those designing these reflected a wider lack of confidence in many NHS librarians around making effective use of metrics. A core focus of KfH is equipping LKS managers with the tools to express the difference their services make. Demonstrating impact is a means for libraries in the NHS to make the case for investment in the context of an organisation where the heart of business is patient care. We need to have things to talk to stakeholders about that make sense to them and help win arguments.

A Task and Finish Group was created within the Quality and Impact work stream to address these issues through building the expertise to support better design and use of metrics. A small geographically distributed group was formed with some changes of membership as other commitments intruded. Working predominantly virtually allowed us to make rapid progress with a single face-to-face meeting required for the final creation of a set of principles for good metrics. We took as our working definition of a metric that "A metric is criteria against which something is measured" (Showers, 2015a, 2015b).

11.4.2 Development of the Principles

The initial focus was to examine the literature around metrics. This was carried out in an opportunistic fashion with a scoping search of the literature and snowball follow-up of interesting papers. We also made use of contacts in other sectors to seek relevant projects and drew on a collation of resources prepared for a SCONUL study on Value and Impact (Evidence Base, 2015).

The recent reference[5] in Higher Education proved a useful source of debate around appropriate construction and use of metrics. The Metric Tide (Wilsdon et al., 2015) explored the potential pitfalls from inappropriate applications of metrics. They created a list of dimensions for responsible metrics including robustness, humility, and transparency. Key documents were also the thorough and highly structured approaches from the British Standards Institute (BSI) (British Standards Institute, 2014) and Health and Social Care Information Centre (since renamed NHS Digital) (Health & Social Care Information Centre, 2017). These gave confidence that we had all the major factors to consider available to us by providing

[5] Research Excellence Framework http://www.ref.ac.uk/.

extensive, carefully defined, lists of criteria for an acceptable metric. These very full lists were felt to be somewhat intimidating and hence a barrier to everyday application but they informed our own synthesis of the principles we were identifying throughout the literature.

A further strand of research was into previous attempts to introduce metrics in NHS LKS. Tools currently, and previously, in use for examining service quality and reporting activity were identified. These were reviewed as a means to understand what made them more or less effective both for understanding services and as a means of engaging stakeholders. This had the added advantage of grounding our discussion in models that are already well understood by our key audience of LKS managers.

An attempt was made to introduce national Key Performance Indicators in 2011. Six potential metrics were consulted on with feedback highlighting issues around their lack of meaning, burdensome data collection, variation in methods, and the potential for gaming/perverse incentives. A set of revised proposals were subsequently made but not adopted.

National statistics returns have been in place in NHS LKS for over two decades. These provide a good data set and extensive practical experience as they are returned by over 80% of services. Issues flagged by examining the returns data include challenges around differing definitions of registered users, enquiry activity, and questionable accuracy for hard to collect data. A concern was the extent to which this data reports busyness without offering any means to understand impact. Many of the figures collected were felt to be of little relevance, or interest, to most stakeholders (including the LKS Managers themselves).

We were keen to get LKS managers thinking about their use of metrics and to gain an understanding of those already in use within their services. To this end an online survey was distributed to the NHS LKS network in England. Respondents were asked to provide details of metrics they found useful including a brief description of how they were calculated. The survey drew 150 responses but only 47 of these offered a metric (a total of 117 metrics in all) (Fricker & Pratchett, 2015). Nine main reasons for selecting a metric were identified with the majority focussed on usage alone or in combination with attempts to segment by user group. It was interesting to note differing approaches to the same sources of data. This offers the possibility of future sharing to establish good practice around a particular metric.

Having completed our research we convened a meeting at which we debated the merits of the approaches discovered and created our own synthesis in the form of four principles for quality metrics.

Meaningful – does the metric relate to the goals of the organisation, to the needs of the users, and is it re-examined over time for continuing appropriateness?

Actionable – is the metric in areas that the LKS can affect? Does it drive a change in behaviour? The reasons for changes to metric should be investigated not assumed.

Reproducible – the metric must be clearly defined in advance of use and transparent. It should be able to be replicated over time and constructed with the most robust data available. Collection of data for the metric should not be burdensome to allow repetition when required.

Comparable – the metric can be used internally by the LKS over time and externally to benchmark against similar services. The diversity of services must be respected.

The desire was for an approachable list of principles that could be readily applied by LKS managers to structure their thinking. To support practical implementation of the principles we created a quality metrics template inspired by a presentation used at Grand River Hospital (Dashboard Spy, 2011). A completed template offers the possibility of easy sharing with other interested parties both within the creator's organisation and other LKS staff seeking to create metrics in similar areas.

Following the release of our report (Metrics Task & Finish Group, 2016) the template was tested during a group workshop at the Health Libraries Group[6] 2016 conference in Scarborough. While those present reported the template to be helpful it was felt that labelling could be clearer and that worked examples would be vital to help adoption. A revised version was created in early 2017 reducing the number of sections to complete while providing more detailed guidance. Contact was also made with Grand River Hospital who have continued to develop their tools and were pleased to hear of our own developments.

---

[6] Chartered Institute for Library and Information Professionals – Health Libraries Group https://www.cilip.org.uk/about/special-interest-groups/health-libraries-group.

Case Study: Experimenting With the Metrics Template - Tracey Pratchett

I joined the Task and Finish group because I'd always struggled to define which metrics were the most relevant to our service and at this time, I also had to revisit our internal quality framework, compiled by my predecessor. I took the decision to completely revamp the format and structure using what I had learned from the Task and Finish Group. The revised document is succinct and outlines our external and internal monitoring requirements, our methods for assessing quality, and key quality standards and performance indicators.

The idea that all library metrics should be meaningful, actionable, reproducible, and comparable, really helped to focus my mind. Once our team had identified the quality standards most important to us at that point in time, I used the template as a platform to analyse each in more detail. Mapping each standard to key drivers, such as our external monitoring process, LQAF (the NHS Library Quality Assurance Framework), really helped me to articulate why each standard was particularly important for our service.

Having space to record *how* the standard was measured, ensures that we are consistently measuring the same things, in the same way each year. This was particularly important for our literature searches which are reported annually but where the collection and reporting methods are slightly different. Adapting the template to include this information means that we can report consistently. After testing the template for my Quality Framework, I also fed my experience back to the Task and Finish Group and the template was tweaked, making it more user friendly.

Our Quality Framework is now published on our website (Pratchett, 2016), explicitly outlining our quality 'promise' to our stakeholders. We also use it to monitor our performance annually which is reported in our annual report and to the Board via the Education and Training Committee. Recently, when our division needed to pull together key standards, having the Quality Framework to hand enabled me to contribute. I also shared the document with nonlibrary colleagues as the principle that all metrics should be meaningful, actionable, reproducible, and comparable is relevant to all services, not just libraries.

11.5 ONGOING DEVELOPMENT OF METRICS IN NHS LKS

A metrics bank is now starting to be populated at http://kfh. libraryservices.nhs.uk to allow for the sharing and refining of metrics in use. This takes the form of a simple online form for submission of templates.

Over time it will create a public resource. It mirrors a similar collection tool being used for sharing case studies around impact. A network of people review submissions and can return them to the submitter if more detail is required to make them readily comprehensible and hence fully useful. This process can potentially also provide helpful guidance to strengthen the quality of a metric as it is brought into use locally. The intention is to publicise metrics that are felt particularly useful through KfH communications channels.

Learning the lesson of previous KPI exercises the intention is not to impose standard metrics across NHS LKS but to allow local managers to consider if a version of a particular metric might be useful for them. The national annual statistics return is to be reviewed and will be influenced by the metrics principles. A number of data points currently collected fail to qualify as good metrics and are therefore likely to be reconsidered. LKS can, of course, choose to continue to collect any data they find useful locally even if it is dropped from national returns.

The direction of travel has been set towards more NHS LKS being better able to confidently define, share, and work with metrics.

11.6 KPI CASE STUDY AT THE PENNSYLVANIA STATE UNIVERSITY

Daniel Coughlin, Joseph Salem Jr., Pennsylvania State University, State College, PA, United States.

In order to analyse the value of a service provided by the libraries it is necessary to create specific metrics to guide this analysis. The values of these metrics, sometimes referred to as key performance indicators (KPIs), indicate the health or worth of the service and potentially impact decisions towards future investment.

The Pennsylvania State University Libraries uses KPIs in evaluating several new and growing initiatives. Digital collections, for example, rely on KPIs for decisions related to continued investment in digitisation and access. In addition to typical usage statistics including downloads and page views, increasingly, digital collection strategists at Penn State use curricular or programmatic integrations of the collections to decide on whether to continue to digitise a collection, enhance access to it, or shift focus to another collection.

Similar to digital collections, repository services and scholarly communication services use KPIs in addition to usage data. In both cases, the primary KPI is the use of the services and resources provided by discipline.

Since both provide their own unique opportunities for different disciplines, examining disciplinary integration of these services facilitates targeted outreach and in some cases the development of additional services.

Over the last 2 years, the teaching and learning program has moved to a KPI model to inform the strategic development of curricular partnerships. Like the services discussed earlier, disciplinary integration is one KPI, with the additional criterion of selecting those integrations to be strategic points in the curricula of each discipline. Additionally, the effectiveness of each key strategic integration is a significant KPI. For teaching and learning, this is measured through assessment of student learning. A recent example includes the rubric-based assessment of student learning in a key point in the Marketing curriculum, with upcoming initiatives focused on general education.

For emerging initiatives like the University Libraries' role in the Penn State Open Educational Resources (OER) and affordable course content program, a set of KPIs was agreed upon at the onset. The goal of the program at Penn State is to reduce course costs for students. Although several KPIs have been useful, including the number of courses converted to open or more affordable course content options, the number of students benefitting from the program, and the number of faculty involved, all KPIs in this case are most useful in determining the primary KPI; the saving to students facilitated by the program (Dewey et al., 2016).

The use of KPIs is most fully developed at Penn State in the area of collection development and strategy. The Pennsylvania State University Libraries spend over 10 million dollars annually on electronic resource subscriptions. These subscriptions provide online access to scholarly articles that are served from outside vendors and/or publishers. The inability to provide access to journals locally is a microcosm of a larger complication in managing and creating KPIs to evaluate journals because this usage or download data is not stored locally at the university.

There has been preliminary work around using several electronic resource key performance indicators such as cost per download, funding area, the amount of times researchers at our university cite a journal, and the amount of times researchers at our university publish in a journal. Additionally, we use Web of Science metrics such as Impact Factor and Eigenfactor to provide a broad view of the significance a journal may have with the larger research community.

Each of these metrics provides different methods for assessing the value of a journal. We have found that the metrics from Web of Science are useful to get a base-level understanding but alone they are not able to accurately predict the value a journal may have at a university. A more accurate way to determine what journals will be used/downloaded at a university is to combine these metrics provided on a more broad-scale view of usage (i.e. Impact Factor) with locally relevant metrics such as number of times researchers at your university cite these journals (Coughlin & Jansen, 2016).

Additionally, although it is not subject-level specific, analysing the funding area can give an assessment by creating a domain area for analysing electronic resources. This creates an ability to establish lines of separation prior to comparison to avoid evaluating journal downloads, for example, in Physical and Mathematical Sciences with those in Arts & Humanities.

The metrics indicated here from Web of Science were created with the intention of evaluating journals for local assessment; however, we must create our own metrics for evaluation because:

(1) Larger, more broad metrics do not include all of the electronic resources we provide access to. In order to be comprehensive we must have our own evaluation in regards to impact and value outcomes within our university.

(2) It can be a poor assumption that the value of an electronic resource broadly will be the value of an electronic resource to the local scholars at this university.

In order to equitably compare journals we can categorise them by funding area to get a sense of what audience they serve. This is currently the easiest way to make this categorisation of electronic resources. The distinction of audience served is important because it levels the playing field making sure our comparison is 'apples to apples'. For example, journals in some fields are not used as often as others. Additionally, when looking at these evaluations to determine what journals may or may not have a subscription renewed it is valuable to know how many other journals serve a particular domain (Coughlin, Campbell, & Jansen, 2016).

Combining metrics we create based on citations at Penn State, with those provided to us by Web of Science, we can create regression models to predict a range of usage for electronic resources. Having the ability to accurately predict a range for usage/downloads of an electronic resource provides an ability to create a price per download we are willing to pay. The creation of an acceptable price range to pay for a journal provides library decision makers with the ability to determine if a journal is accurately priced, a bargain, or overpriced.

We would not make decisions based solely on this quantitative analysis; however, these KPI provide us with outliers that we can further evaluate.

There are too many electronic resources to evaluate all of them, so by finding those that need further evaluation we can more accurately assess those materials and ensure we are providing access to journals that provide value for scholars of all disciplines.

11.7 CASE STUDIES SUMMARY

The five case studies included in this chapter effectively illustrate key performance indicators in practice in a number of different library and information settings. Using a mix of higher education and health library sector libraries the case studies bring to life some of the thinking and planning that goes into setting KPIs and how they need to align to strategy and outcomes. It is also interesting to see how most of the case study examples are not using true KPIs per se, but are responding to their parent organisations and reporting on the measures and indicators that contribute to the success and the outcomes of the institution. Interestingly, the two UK-based university case studies both site Customer Service Excellence, an outward facing kite mark, as being instrumental in determining some of the measures that they report and cleverly use some of the outward facing customer service standards as KPIs in different contexts. In the case of Kingston University the library service is using a clear metric (that of student satisfaction – an annual target) as a result indicator, but are using some of their customer service standards, which they are measuring more frequently as key performance indicators in order to forecast how they will do against the key result indicator of the National Student Survey satisfaction score. The example of Liverpool John Moores University suggests that, potentially a more balanced Scorecard approach is taking place where all activity is measured, including staff training and development and appropriate performance indicators have been identified accordingly. Likewise the McMaster case study presents a similar scenario in Canada and a strategic approach to defining and measuring key performance indicators through a balanced Scorecard.

The case study by Fricker and Pratchett is fascinating in that it discusses a very ambitious initiative, that of defining a set of key performance indicators for a national health care organisation and illustrates the challenges of getting buy-in and agreement to a common set of indicators across an entire sector. The final case study from Pennsylvania State University shows how KPIs can be applied to specific areas of the library and information service and in this case to the digital collections service. This approach is particularly useful in that the performance indicators discussed, whilst in some cases are usage metrics, have been selected as specific indicators towards the key result, that of reducing the cost of the programme of study to the student.

It is hoped that these case studies have helped to illustrate how some of the narrative and theory behind performance measurement and key performance indicators are applied in practice in real library and information settings. What is most interesting is the valuation that there is no one way of defining and applying key performance indicators and how the theory is interpreted and how different metrics are used as measures differ from institution to institution and from sector to sector. In essence if the measure chosen does indeed indicate that a strategic objective or an outcome is being achieved, then it can be regarded as a key performance indicator.

CHAPTER TWELVE

Using KPIs in Your Library and Information Service

This chapter will bring together some of the examples of Key Performance Indicators identified in Chapter 11 and will present, in a simple list form some indicative performance indicators that could be used and applied in different library and information service settings. For the purposes of this book they have been laid out in just two sections: academic libraries and public libraries. Although only indicative, the KPIs suggested are transferable and anybody using this list as a framework for developing their own KPIs is advised to look through both sections and make use of any suggested indicators that they think are relevant to their own library and information environment. They are designed to provide you with ideas and suggestions as to how you might form an indicator around the anticipated outcomes, targets, and strategic objectives of your own library service. Don't forget that the indictors that you use need to relate to your strategies and the intended outcomes of your service. This is not the same for each library service or library sector.

12.1 ACADEMIC LIBRARIES

Strategic Driver or Anticipated Outcome	Possible Key Performance Indicator
Supporting the Student Experience	• % of Library Critical Friends members who feel their engagement with the forum has made a difference to services • % of open day attendees who attend library tours • % increase in usage stats of alumni
Supporting Learning and Teaching activities of the university	• % of PCs available at certain point throughout the day • % reading list items available in the library • % reading list items available electronically

Libraries and Key Performance Indicators
http://dx.doi.org/10.1016/B978-0-08-100227-8.00012-1

- % of curriculum areas engaging with reading list initiatives
- Variance rate between print and e-resources (becoming increasingly favourable towards e-resource)
- Length of time taken to fix out of order PCs
- % of Library Services staff with Higher Education Academy (HEA) accreditation or similar
- Satisfaction rating in the National Student Survey
- % satisfaction with user education sessions
- % of face-to-face enquiries referred to other colleagues
- % of telephone enquiries closed at the point of first contact
- % students who do not engage with Library Services

Supporting Research and Scholarship

- % increase of items placed in the institutional repository
- % items in repository cited in further research
- Use of Research Data Management Services
- Page Views from RDM website
- % increase in consultations/visits to Special Collections and Archives
- % increase in PhD studentships based on library collections and archives
- Library participation in joint (university or external) grant proposals
- % of successful joint grant proposals

Supporting/increasing distance education

- % increase in off campus usage of library resources
- Usage e-resources by marginal students (widening participation)
- % increase/decrease in access to library resources from overseas

Developing digital collections

- Page Views from the Digital Archive
- % increase in digitised Items uploaded to the Digital Archive
- % increase in number of books digitised

Community engagement

- % increase of external exhibitions with which to include contributions from library special collections and archives

	• % increase of visitors to internal exhibitions • % visitors to internal exhibitions who would rate the exhibition 'good' or 'excellent' in exit survey
Staff Resources/Staff Development	• % staff who have completed a performance review within the last 12 months • % staff who have attended internal training • % staff who have attended bespoke training session • Retention rates of library staff after 1 and 5 years of recruiting

12.2 PUBLIC LIBRARIES

Strategic Driver or Anticipated Outcome	Possible Key Performance Indicator
Supporting community cohesion	• % of Friends of the Library Group members who feel their engagement with the forum has made a difference to services • Number/% increase of reading group attendees • Number/% increase of library users attending 'friendship groups'/'knit and natter', etc. • Number of new library user registrations following 'family fun day' • Number/% increase of library users satisfied with access and opening hours • Number/% increase in job seekers finding employment through library information channels • Number/% increase in library users successfully finding health information through library information channels • Number/% increase in library users successfully accessing government or local authority services through library information channels

Reading and literacy	• % increase of print materials borrowed by age range
	• Number of bilingual reading items available in the library
	• Number/% increase in reading group attendees
	• Increase in regional literacy rates
Supporting the development of children and young people	• Number/% increase of under 16 library registrations
	• Number/% increase in attendance at homework clubs
	• Number/% increase in attendance at coding clubs
	• Number/% increase in attendance at 'story time'
	• Number of recommendations for stock (from children/young people)
	• Usage statistics of children's collections
	• Number of young people studying in the library
Digital inclusion	• Number/% increase in attendance at digital skills workshops
	• Number/% increase in library users having completed digital skills workshops
	• Number/% increase in library users having gained digital skills certificates
	• Number/% increase in library users considering themselves 'digitally literate'
	• Number/% increase of networked PCs/laptops/tablets available for library users to use
	• Usage statistics of networked PCs/laptops/tablets
	• Number/% increase of library users registering for follow-up courses
Community engagement	• % increase of library registrations through new visitors to the library
	• % increase of visitors to internal exhibitions
	• % visitors to internal exhibitions who would rate the exhibition 'good' or 'excellent' in exit survey
	• Number/% increase of 'Learn My Way' courses completed

Services for users with disabilities	• Number/% increase of library users declaring disabilities • Number/% increase of users engaging with specialist software • % increase in satisfaction with library from users with disabilities users • % increase in number of books digitised
Enabling social networking	• Number/% increase of reading group attendees • Number/% increase of library users attending 'friendship groups'/'knit and natter', etc.
Staff Resources/Staff Development	• % staff who have completed a performance review within the last 12 months • % staff who have attended training as part of rolling programme • % staff who have attended bespoke training session • Retention rates of library staff after 1 and 5 years of recruiting • Retention rates of library volunteers/ digital mentors

CHAPTER THIRTEEN

Final Reflections Performance Measurement and Performance Indicators

One of the intentions of this book was to try to bring some clarity and understanding to the concept of using performance indicators and key performance indicators within a performance measurement environment for library and information services. There has always been confusion and disagreement as to what exactly is meant by a key performance indicator, and the terminology is often misused, not just in the library and information sector, but across a whole variety of government, nonprofit, and commercial organisations. It could be argued that rather than clarify what is meant by a KPI, through discussing and unpicking library KPIs within a performance measurement setting has actually made things all the more confusing.

However, what has become clear, is that the underlying principle and main intention of applying KPIs, is that the organisation is trying to be accountable and is trying to report back on the quality of their service through metrics and other measures. Measuring performance is important to libraries. It is how they find out what needs to be improved or further developed. It is how they are responsive services to their users. It is how they celebrate success and make cases for sustained or increased finding to improve service further still. But this was not always the case. There was a time when libraries did not need to measure performance for accountability and in order to inform improvements, but rather they counted their transactions and monitored their usage. This was still for planning purposes, but was more inclined to be measures of how busy (or not) or how well used (or not) as service was in comparison to other services. The library user was not regarded as an agent in this.

By taking a systematic approach to how KPIs have come about and how they are used as tool in modern library and information service performance measurement, the opening chapters of the book have taken a look at different elements of performance measurement and have illustrated several quantitative, qualitative, and mixed methods used for performance measurement

Libraries and Key Performance Indicators
http://dx.doi.org/10.1016/B978-0-08-100227-8.00013-3

and service evaluation. These sections are not intended to act as any kind of guide book or manual, this is achieved far more effectively in several other publications. The reason, however, that it has been necessary to look in some detail at the history of performance measurement in libraries is to be able to fully understand how we have arrived at the need and desire to measure performance through performance indicators and KPIs.

By looking at library performance measurement in this way, and particularly the impact and influence that 'new managerialism' has had on the performance measurement of libraries it allows us to see a transformation in libraries, in general, from collection-oriented services to more customer focused and oriented services. This really stands out in much of the recent literature which talks about measuring performance in order to evidence value for money to the customer or to ensure visibility of service improvements by sharing with customers how well it is doing. This is apparent in some of case studies later in the book, where a real driver to develop and implement KPIs and remain accountable to them has been associated with achieving external 'customer service' recognition through awards such as Customer Service Excellence or the Charter Mark. Being able to report back to users as to how a library is reaching its targets and standards is now very much a feature of many library services and subsequently customer service standards become more and more common and tend to double as performance indicators. This is appropriate if the numbers in question to indicate movement towards the end 'goal'. The latter chapters of the book discuss 'outcomes' of library usage as being significant with regard to how the performance of a service is measured. This is particularly important where libraries are asked to demonstrate the impact and value that they have on their users. In order to demonstrate impact and value, a library needs to be explicit as to its desired outcomes and these can be articulated through strategic documents such as strategic plans and library vision statements. This then allows us to look at how a service can attempt to measure its performance against its outcomes using a variety of already established quantitative and qualitative methods.

It is the area of 'measuring outcomes' which allows for the further discussion of performance indicators and KPIs, as these can be used as periodic indicators against the intended 'end result' or outcome. By introducing some of the well known KPI commentators and writers, such as David Parmenter and Bernard Marr, we have been able to look at developing and implementing KPIs slightly more objectively than if we were to just look at what is written in the library and information science literature. Some of the guidance and illustration about how KPIs can be developed and implemented and their importance to strategic objectives should be useful to library managers. This is supplemented by a series of illuminative case studies and some further indicative, suggested KPIs intended to provide inspiration and ideas for individual library managers to start to think about developing their own KPIs for their own services.

Being able to take time to look specifically at KPIs in library and information environments and where they sit in the culture of performance measurement in which we now operate has been refreshing. It is good to see that library and information service want to be accountable and want to perform at high levels. Being able to measure what they do is important in this environment and there are a plethora of ways in which they can approach this, from the quantitative and qualitative methods discussed, to setting and reporting on challenging customer service standards. Key Performance Indicators form a vital part of this toolkit and should be used to see 'at a glance' how well the library is achieving its goals.

In summary, in setting KPIs, in order for them to be effective, library managers need to ask themselves the following three things:

- What is the library trying to achieve? (outcome)
- If achieved successfully, what will that success look like? (outcome)
- What find of measurement can I take along the way to check that we're going in the right direction? (performance indicator or KPI)

REFERENCES

Aabo, S., & Audunsen, R. (2002). Rational choice and valuation of public libraries: Can economic models for evaluating non-market goods be applied to public libraries? *Journal of Library and Information Science, 34*(1), 5–16.

Anderson, R. (2010). Scholarly communications: The view from the library. In L. Estelle & H. Woodward (Eds.), *Digital information: Order or anarchy* (pp. 35–56). London: Facet Publishing.

Audit Commission. (2009). *Comprehensive area assessment framework.* http://archive.auditcommission.gov.uk/auditcommission/SiteCollectionDocuments/MethodologyAndTools/Guidance/caaframework10feb09REP.pdf (Accessed 2 October 2013).

Bell, S. (2010). The reference user Ex: Fish market 101: Why not a reference user experience? *Library Journal, 15*, 6–7.

Berg, B. (2009). *Qualitative research methods for the social sciences* (7th ed.). Boston, MA: Allyn and Bacon.

Bertot, J. C. (2004). Libraries and networked information services: Issues and consideration in measurement. *Performance Measurement and Metrics, 5*(1), 11–19.

Blagden, J., & Harrington, J. (1990). *How good is your library? A review of approaches to the evaluation of library and information services.* London: Aslib.

Bloor, M., Frankland, J., Thomas, M., & Robson, K. (2002). *Focus groups in social research.* London: Sage.

Bloor, M., & Wood, F. (2006). *Keywords in qualitative methods: A vocabulary of research concepts.* London: Sage.

Bradford, S. C. (1948). *Documentation.* London: Crosby-Lockwood.

British Standards Institute. (2008). *Information and documentation—Library performance indicators: BS ISO 11620:2008.* London: British Standards Institute.

British Standards Institute. (2014). *BS ISO 11620:2014—Information and documentation. Library performance indicators.* London: British Standards Institute.

Broady-Preston, J., & Lobo, A. (2011). Measuring the quality, value and impact of academic libraries: The role of external standards. *Performance Measurement and Metrics, 12*(2), 122–135.

Brophy, P. (2001). *The library in the twenty-first century: New services for the information age.* London: Library Association Publishing.

Brophy, P. (2006). *Measuring library performance: Principles and techniques.* London: Facet Publishing.

Brown, M. (2014). Is altmetrics an acceptable replacement for citation counts and the impact factor. *The Serials Librarian, 67*, 27–30.

Bryant, J., Matthews, G., & Walton, G. (2009). Academic libraries and social learning space: A case study of Loughborough University Library, UK. *Journal of Librarianship and Information Science, 41*(1), 7–18.

Buchanan, S., & Salako, A. (2009). Evaluating the usability and usefulness of a digital library. *Library Review, 58*(9), 638–651.

Campbell, J. (2013). *The library: A world history.* London: Thames & Hudson.

Carr, R. (2006). *What users want: An academic 'hybrid' library perspective. Ariadne. 46.* http://www.ariadne.ac.uk/issue46/carr/ (Accessed 12 December 2014).

Carter, N., Klein, R., & Day, P. (1995). *How organisations measure success: The use of performance indicators in government.* London: Routledge.

Cave, M., Hanney, S., Henkel, M., & Kogan, M. (1997). *The use of performance indicators in higher education: The challenge of the quality movement* (3rd ed.). London: Jessica Kingsley Publishers.

Chowhdury, G., Burton, P., McMenemy, D., & Pulter, A. (2008). *Librarianship: An introduction*. London: Facet Publishing.

Corrall, S. (2000). *Strategic management of information services: A planning handbook*. London: Aslib.

Coughlin, D. M., Campbell, M. C., & Jansen, B. J. (2016). A web analytics approach for appraising electronic resources in academic libraries. *Journal of the Association of Information Science Technology, 67*(3), 518–534.

Coughlin, D. M., & Jansen, B. J. (2016). Modeling journal bibliometrics to predict downloads and inform purchase decisions at university research libraries. *Journal of the Association of Information Science Technology, 67*(9), 2263–2273.

Crawford, J. (2000). *Evaluation of library and information services* (2nd ed.). London: Aslib Publishing.

Crawford, J. (2006). *The culture of evaluation in library and information services*. Oxford: Chandos.

Dashboard Spy. (2011). *Hospital dashboard project*. Retrieved from http://dashboardspy.com/tag/mckesson-hbi/ (Accessed 28 January 2017).

De La Mano, M., & Creaser, C. (2014). The impact of the balanced scorecard in libraries: From performance measurement to strategic management. *Journal of Library and Information Science, 48*(2), 191–208.

Delcore, H. D., Mullooly, J., Scroggins, M., Arnold, K., Franco, E., & Gaspar, J. (2009). *The library study at Fresno State*. Retrieved from http://www.fresnostate.edu/socialsciences/anthropology/ipa/thelibrarystudy.html.

Dent-Goodman, V. (2011). *Qualitative research and the modern library*. Oxford: Chandos.

Dewey, B. I., Salem, J. A., Davidson, E., Aebli, F., Domico, K., & Falke, S. (2016). *Open educational resources (OER) task force report*. University Park, PA: Pennsylvania State University. 40 p. Report No: 1.

Dowd, F. S. (1996). Homeless children in public libraries: A national survey of large systems. *Journal of Youth Services in Libraries, 9*(2), 155–166.

Duff, A. (2013). *A normative theory of the information society*. New York, NY: Routledge.

Duke, L. M., & Asher, A. D. (Eds.), (2012). *College libraries and student culture: What we now know*. Chicago, IL: American Library Association.

European Commission. (2013). *Investing in European success: Horizon 2020: Research and innovation to boost growth and jobs in Europe*. Luxembourg: Publications Office of the European Union.

Evidence Base. (2015). *SCONUL value and impact pinboard*. Retrieved from https://pinboard.in/t:sconulvalueandimpact/ (Accessed 27 January 2017).

Feather, J. (2013). *The information society: A study of continuity and change* (6th ed.). London: Facet Publishing.

Feather, J., & Sturges, P. (Eds.), (1997). *International encyclopaedia of information and library science*. New York, NY: Routledge.

Finch Group (Working Group on Expanding Access to Published Research Findings). (2012). *Accessibility, sustainability, excellence: How to expand access to research publications*. Creative Commons. http://www.researchinfonet.org/wp-content/uploads/2012/06/Finch-Group-report-FINAL-VERSION.pdf (Accessed 17 February 2013).

Foster, N. F., & Gibbons, S. (2007). Studying students: The undergraduate research project. In N. F. Foster & S. Gibbons (Eds.), *Library*. Chicago, IL: Association of College and Research Libraries. Retrieved from http://www.ala.org/acrl/sites/ala.org.acrl/files/content/publications/booksanddigitalresources/digital/Foster-Gibbons_cmpd.pdf.

Franklin, B., & Plum, T. (2008). Assessing the value and impact of digital content. *Journal of Library Administration, 48*(1), 41–58.

Fricker, A., & Pratchett, T. (2015). *Considering metrics for NHS library services*. Retrieved from http://www.slideshare.net/AlanFricker/considering-metrics-for-nhs-library-services (Accessed 29 January 2017).

Gorman, G. E., & Clayton, P. (2005). *Qualitative research for the information professional: A practical handbook* (2nd ed.). London: Facet Publishing.

Goulding, A. (2004). Libraries and social capital. *Journal of Librarianship and Information Science, 36*(1), 3–6.

Greatbanks, R., & Tapp, D. (2001). The impact of balanced scorecards in a public sector environment: Empirical evidence from Dunedin City Council. *International Journal of Operations and production Management, 27*(8), 846–873.

Groombridge, B. (1964). *The Londoner and his library*. London: The Research Institute for Consumer Affairs.

Health and Social Care Information Centre. (2017). *National library of quality assurance indicators*. Retrieved from http://www.hscic.gov.uk/article/5175/Library (Accessed 28 January 2017).

Health Education England. (2014). *Knowledge for healthcare: A development framework for NHS library and knowledge services in England 2015–2020*. London: Health Education England.

Hernon, P., & Altman, E. (2010). *Assessing service quality: Satisfying the expectations of library customers*. Chicago, IL: American Library Association.

Hernon, P., Altman, E., & Dugan, R. (2015). *Assessing service quality: Satisfying the expectations of library customers* (3rd ed.). London: Facet Publishing.

Hernon, P., & Whitman, J. R. (2001). *Delivering satisfaction and service quality*. Chicago, IL: American Library Association.

Hoeppner, A. (2012). The ins and outs of evaluating web-scale discovery services. *Computers in Libraries, 32*(3). 6–10, 38–40.

Holmes, A., & Parsons, F. (2016). The institutional HE quality perspective. In J. Atkinson (Ed.), *Quality and the academic library: Reviewing, assessing and enhancing provision* (pp. 17–26). London: Chandos.

Huysmans, F., & Oomes, M. (2013). Measuring the public library's societal value: A methodological research programme. *IFLA Journal, 39*(2), 168–177.

International Organisation for Standardisation. (2014). *ISO 11620:2014—Information and documentation. Library performance indicators* (3rd ed.). Geneva: ISO.

Johnes, J., & Taylor, J. (1990). *Performance indicators in higher education: UK universities*. Buckingham: Society for Research into Higher Education.

Kaplan, R. (1999). The balances scorecard for public sector organisations. *The Balances Scorecard Report: Insight, experience and ideas for strategy focused organisations: Vol. 1, no. 2*.

Kaplan, R. S., & Norton, D. P. (1986). *The balanced scorecard: Translating strategy into action*. Boston, MA: Harvard Business School Press.

Kaplan, R., & Norton, D. (1996). *The balanced scorecard: Translating strategy into action*. Boston, MA: Harvard Business School Press.

Kerslake, E., & Kinnel, M. (1997). *The social impact of public libraries: A literature review*. London: British Library.

Kingston University. (2012). *Led by learning*. http://www.kingston.ac.uk/aboutkingstonuniversity/howtheuniversityworks/universityplan/ (Accessed 31 January 2017).

Krueger, R., & Casey, M. -A. (2009). *Focus Groups: A practical guide for applied research* (4th ed.). Los Angeles, CA: Sage.

Kyrillidou, M. (2010). The ARL library scorecard pilot: Using the balanced scorecard in research libraries. *Research Library Issues, 271*, 33–35.

Lancaster, F. W. (1993). *If you want to evaluate your library…* (2nd ed.). Champaign, IL: University of Illinois.

Lancaster, F. W., & Jonich, M. J. (1977). *The measurement and evaluation of library services*. Washington, DC: Information Resources Press.

Lapinski, S., Piwowar, H., & Priem, J. (2013). Riding the crest of the altmetric wave: How librarians can help prepare faculty for the next generation of research impact metrics. *College and Research Libraries News, 74*(6), 292–300.

Linley, R., & Usherwood, B. (1998). *New measures for the new library: A social audit of public libraries (British Library Research and Innovation Centre report; 89)*. Sheffield: Centre for the Public Library in the Information Society, University of Sheffield.

Luther, J. (2008). *University investment in the library: What's the return?: A case study at the University of Illinois at Urban-Champaign*. Library Connect. White paper 1.

Mackenzie, A. (2016). Reviewing the value of the SCONUL statistics: A case study. In J. Atkinson (Ed.), *Quality and the academic library: Reviewing, assessing and enhancing provision* (pp. 191–194). London: Chandos.

Markless, S., & Streatfield, D. (2005). Facilitating the impact implementation programme. *Library and Information Research, 29*(91), 8–13.

Markless, S., & Streatfield, D. (2006). *Evaluating the impact of your library*. London: Facet Publishing.

Marr, B. (2014). *25 need-to-know key performance indicators*. Harlow: Pearson.

Marr, B. (2015a). *Big data: Using smart big data, analytics and metrics to make better decisions and improve performance*. Chichester: Wiley.

Marr, B. (2015b). *Key performance indicators for dummies*. Chichester: Wiley.

Marshall, J. (2007). Measuring the value and impact of health library and information services: Past reflections, future possibilities. *Health Information and Libraries Journal, 24*(Suppl. 1), 4–17.

Mattelart, A. (2003). *The information society: An introduction*. London: Sage.

Matthews, J. R. (2008). *Scorecards for results: A guide for developing a library balanced scorecard*. Westport, CT: Libraries Unlimited.

Mays, R., Tenopir, C., & Kaufman, P. (2010). Lib-Value: Measuring value and return on investment of academic libraries. *Research Library Issues: A Bi-monthly Report From ARL, CNI, and SPARC, 271*, 36–40.

McMenemy, D. (2009). *The public library*. London: Facet Publishing.

Metrics Task and Finish Group. (2016). *Principles for metrics—Report and recommendations*. Retrieved from http://kfh.libraryservices.nhs.uk/wp-content/uploads/2016/04/Metrics-Principles-Report-Final-2016.pdf (Accessed 28 January 2017).

Morgan, D. (1997). *Focus groups as qualitative research*. Thousand Oaks, CA: Sage.

Morse, P. M. (1968). *Library effectiveness*. Boston, MA: MIT Press.

Munde, G., & Marks, K. (2009). *Surviving the future; Academic libraries, quality, and assessment*. Oxford: Chandos.

Nachimas, D., & Worth-Nachimas, C. (2008). *Research methods in the social sciences* (7th ed.). New York, NY: Worth Publishers.

Orr, R. H. (1973). Measuring the goodness of library services: A general framework for considering quantitative measures. *Journal of Documentation, 29*(3), 41–50.

Parmenter, D. (2010). *Key performance indicators: Developing, implementing, and using winning KPIs*. New York, NY: Wiley.

Parmenter, D. (2012). *Key performance indicators for government and non profit agencies: Implementing winning KPIs*. New York, NY: Wiley.

Payne, P., & Conyers, A. (2005). Measuring the impact of higher education libraries. *Library and Information Research, 29*(91), 3–7.

Pickard, A. (2006). *Research methods in information*. London: Facet Publishing.

Poll, R. (2001). Performance, processes and costs: Managing service quality with the balanced scorecard. *Library Trends, 49*(4), 709–717.

Poll, R. (2003a). Impact/outcome measures for libraries. *LIBER Quarterly, 13*, 329–342.

Poll, R. (2003b). Measuring impact and outcomes of libraries. *Performance Measurement and Metrics, 4*(1), 5–12.

Poll, R., & Payne, P. (2006). Impact measures for library and information services. *Library Hi Tech, 24*(4), 547–557.

Poll, R., & te Boekhorst, P. (2007). *Measuring quality: Performance measurement in libraries* (2nd ed. Revised). Durban: IFLA Publications.

Pratchett, T. (2016). *Quality framework 2016–2019*. Retrieved from http://healthacademy. lancsteachinghospitals.nhs.uk/library-about-us (Accessed 18 February 2017).

Priem, J. (2014). Altmetrics. In B. Cronin & C. Sugimoto (Eds.), *Beyond bibliometrics: Harnessing multidimensional indicators of scholarly impact* (pp. 263–288). Cambridge, MA: MIT Press.

Priestner, A. (2015). UXLibs: A new breed of conference. *Cilip Update*, (May), 31–33.

Priestner, A., & Borg, M. (2016). Uncovering complexity and detail: The UX proposition. In A. Priestner & M. Borg (Eds.), *User experience in libraries: Applying ethnography and human-centred design* (pp. 1–8). London: Routledge.

Pritchard, A. (1969). Statistical bibliography or bibliometrics? *Journal of Documentation, 25*(4), 348–349.

Pung, C., Clarke, A., & Patten, L. (2004). Measuring the economic impact of the British library. *New Review of Academic Librarianship, 10*(1), 79–102.

Ramsden, B. (2016). Using ethnographic methods to study library use. In A. Priestner & M. Borg (Eds.), *User experience in libraries: Applying ethnography and human-centred design* (pp. 9–20). London: Routledge.

Ranganathan, S. R. (1931). *The five laws of library science*. Madras, India: Madras Library Association.

Revill, D. (1990). *Performance measures for academic libraries. Encyclopedia of library and information science: Vol. 45, Suppl. 10*. New York: Marcel Dekker.

Roberts, S., & Rowley, J. (2004). *Managing information services*. London: Facet Publishing.

Rohm, H. (2004). A balancing act. *Performance Measurement in Action, 2*(2), 1–8.

Rowley, J. (2005). Making sense of the quality maze: Perspectives for public and academic libraries. *Library Management, 26*(8/9), 508–518.

Schmidt, A. (2010). *New column launch: The user experience*. http://www.libraryjournal.com/article/CA6713142.html (Accessed 10 July 2015).

Showers, B. (2015a). *Library analytics and metrics: Using data to drive decisions and services*. London: Facet Publishing.

Showers, B. (2015b). Introduction: Getting the measure of analytics and metrics. In B. Showers (Ed.), *Library analytics and metrics: Using data to drive decisions and services*. London: Facet Publishing.

Slater, M. (1990). *Research methods in library and information studies*. London: Library Association.

Stone, G., Pattern, D., & Ramsden, B. (2012). The library impact data project: Hit, miss or maybe. In: I. Hall, S. Thornton, & S. Town (Eds.), *Proving value in challenging times: Proceedings of the 9th Northumbria international conference on performance measurement in libraries and information services* (pp. 385–390). York: University of York Press.

Suarez, D. (2007). What students do when they study in the library: Using ethnographic methods to observe student behavior. *Electronic Journal of Academic and Special Librarianship, 8*(3), 1–19 Retrieved from http://southernlibrarianship.icaap.org/content/v08n03/suarez_d01.html.

Tenopir, C. (2010). Measuring the value of the academic library: Return on investment and other measures. *The Serials Librarian, 58*, 39–48.

Tenopir, C., & Fleming-May, R. A. (2011). The LibValue Project: Three reports on values, outcomes and return on investment of academic libraries. In *Proceedings of the Charleston Library Conference*.

Totterdell, A. (2005). *An introduction to library and information work*. London: Facet Publishing.

Town, S. (2011). Value, impact, and the transcendent library: Progress and pressures in performance measurement and evaluation. *Library Quarterly, 81*(1), 111–125.

Town, S., & Kyrillidon, M. (2012). Developing a values scorecard. In: I. Hall, S. Thornton, & S. Town (Eds.), *Proving value in challenging times: Proceedings of the 9th Northumbria international conference on performance measurement in libraries and information services*, York: University of York Press, pp. 413–423.

Troll, D. A. (2001). *How and why libraries are changing.* http://old.diglib.org/use/whitepaper.htm (Accessed 17 February 2013; 31 July 2014).

UK Government Cabinet Office (2010). *Customer service excellence the government standard.* www.cse.cabinetoffice.gov.uk/homeCSE.do (Accessed 13 February 2014).

Varheim, A. (2007). Social capital and public libraries: The need for research. *Library and Information Science Research, 29,* 416–428.

Welker, J. (2012). Counting on COUNTER: The current state of e-resource usage data in libraries. *Computers in Libraries, 32*(9), 6–11.

White, C. T. (2009). *Studying students: The ethnographic research project at Rutgers (part 2).* Retrieved from http://www.libraries.rutgers.edu/rul/staff/groups/ethnography/reports/ERP_FinalReport_Phase_2.pdf.

Whitworth, A. (2009). *Information obesity.* Oxford: Chandos.

Wilsdon, J., Allen, L., Belfiore, E., Campbell, P., Curry, S., Hill, S., et al. (2015). *The metric tide: Report of the independent review of the role of metrics in research assessment and management.* HEFCE. Retrieved from http://www.hefce.ac.uk/pubs/rereports/Year/2015/metrictide/Title,104463,en.html (Accessed 28 January 2017).

KINGSTON UNIVERSITY, KEY PERFORMANCE INDICATORS AND SERVICE STANDARDS

KPIS

% of students taught at Kingston University expressing overall satisfaction with the library. To be within 1% of the sector average or greater by 2016.

Information Expenditure per FTE student. Midway towards comparator mean by 2016.

NSS score Q16 – % students agree. Within 1% sector average or greater by 2016.

Student satisfaction with library support for their academic needs. 1% increase annually to 2016.

Student satisfaction with service received within the LRCs. To hold at target satisfaction rate of 95%.

LRC Opening Hours. To meet advertised opening hours.

Information literacy session offered to all campus-based students in level 4 and at their dissertation level. 100% level 4 and 100% dissertation level by 2016.

% of learning resources available in digital formats. Five percent annual increase in eBook collections growing to 46% of total collection by 2016.

SERVICE STANDARDS

	Service Area	Standard
1	Opening hours	We will be open 100% of our advertised opening hours
2	Resource discovery	24/7 access to iCat will be available for at least 98% of the time, averaged across the academic year

3	Resource availability	Self-service facilities will be available for at least 98% of advertised opening hours, averaged across the academic year
4		All open access stock will be readily available in a public area in classmark order within 24 hours or one working day of return
5		At least 80% of printed books and audio-visual items ordered for the LRC will be available within one working day of receipt
6		At least 95% of new e-books to be activated on iCat within three working days of being ordered
7		At least 90% of items requested for digitisation will be made available in the eReserves for academic staff to link to their modules by the required deadline, provided they meet the current copyright licence conditions
8	Help Desk services	Users will wait no more than four minutes at the LRC Help Desk
9	Facilities	At least 95% of LRC computers will be operational during LRC opening hours, averaged across the academic year
10		LRC printing facilities will be operational for at least 98% of the time during LRC opening hours, averaged across the academic year
11		At least 95% engagement with Staff Student Consultative Committees by responding to feedback within five working days of receipt
12		Written (or formal) complaints will be acknowledged within one working day with an aim to respond within three working days. We undertake to consider all complaints seriously and to resolve them satisfactorily whenever possible within the Library. If we are unable to resolve a complaint within the Library we will give details of how it can be progressed further. We aim to progress fewer than five complaints a year

} Library and
} Knowledge Services

NHS
Health Education England

NHS, TEMPLATE TO SUPPORT THE CREATION AND SHARING OF QUALITY METRICS: GMC SURVEY SCORES

The construction of metrics is not a straightforward task. There are many aspects of our services that we can collect data on but not all of these are suitable to be metrics. What works for one situation or stakeholder may not be effective for another. Collection should not be potentially inconsistent or excessively burdensome. We need to be able to influence the future scores through our development and delivery of the service.

To help Library & Knowledge Service Managers to make better use of metrics this template offers both a structure to build your metric and a checklist of principles which make it effective. As you complete the template consider the guidance provided in italics (feel free to delete them once used) – you may not have to answer all of them and there may be other detail you wish to add. Review the checklist – this offers criteria which may further your thinking. Your completed template will provide you with a record that you can review regularly to ensure the metric remains useful. Elements of it can be shared with stakeholders to support engagement and provide assurance. You can modify this template or insert it into other documents as required.

Completing this template also offers a means to share your metric in such a way that others can learn from it and consider adaptation or adoption in their own setting. It has been tested by the Metrics Task and Finish group. A shared collection of metrics will be created from your submissions at http://kfh.libraryservices.nhs.uk/metrics-bank/.

This template was informed by a model prepared by Grand River Hospital who have agreed our use. The principles for good metrics were developed by the Metrics Task and Finish group in their Principles for Metrics Report.

Metric definition:
GMC Survey scores against Access to Educational Resources and sub questions on Library Services, Online Journals and Space for Private Study. Overall score, specialty outliers, positive versus negative satisfaction ratings

Why is it important?
Key score for Medical Education in Trust
High quality national data with good granularity from a core user group (can look at Trust, Site, and Specialty)
Very high participation rate. Consistent year-on-year application
Not Library delivered reducing bias
LQAF sections 1.2e Service development informed by evidence/1.3c Positive impact

Process for compiling the Metric:
Data from GMC Survey site – http://www.gmc-uk.org/education/surveys.asp
 – Overall score for Trust for Access to Educational Resources from Summary page
 – Download scores for individual sub questions (click through the overall Access to the Educational Resources Score)
 – site-by-site data available but some question marks over accuracy of coding to sites
 – Specialty data for outliers should be examined
 – Sentiment analysis by calculating (very good + good) – (very poor + poor) = sentiment score

What does it mean?
Compare performance on different measures year on year
Compare shifts within specialties that have been targeted following red flags in previous years
Compare sites for local issues
Benchmark against equivalent organisations
Be aware of wider issues within Trust/Specialties that may have negative halo

Desired outcomes:
Have useful conversation with Medical Education
Zero red flags for specialties
Improve absolute performance
Improve performance against benchmark Trusts

Improvement plans:
Subject to areas highlighted and research on benchmark services

Reporting:
Results included in annual report. Annual GMS Survey Report prepared for each Trust and discussed at Library User Boards. Annual benchmarking report prepared for Library Leadership Team/wider Library Services

CHECKLIST

Does your metric meet the following criteria?

✓ *Meaningful* – does the metric relate to the goals of the organisation, to the needs of the users and is it re-examined over time for continuing appropriateness? Do other people care about it? Combining two facets can strengthen a metric – for example usage by a particular staff group.

✓ *Actionable* – is the metric in areas that the LKS can influence? Does it drive a change in behaviour? The reasons for changes to a metric should be investigated not assumed. Beware self-imposed targets – are they meaningful to stakeholders?

✓ *Reproducible* – the metric is a piece of research so should be clearly defined in advance of use and transparent. It should be able to be replicated over time and constructed with the most robust data available. Collection of data for the metric should not be burdensome to allow repetition when required.

✓ *Comparable* – the metric can be used to see change in the LKS over time. Be cautious if trying to benchmark externally. The diversity of services must be respected – no one metric fits all.

} Library and
} Knowledge Services

NHS
Health Education England

NHS, TEMPLATE TO SUPPORT THE CREATION AND SHARING OF QUALITY METRICS: LQAF COMPLIANCE

The construction of metrics is not a straightforward task. There are many aspects of our services that we can collect data on but not all of these are suitable to be metrics. What works for one situation or stakeholder may not be effective for another. Collection should not be potentially inconsistent or excessively burdensome. We need to be able to influence the future scores through our development and delivery of the service.

To help Library & Knowledge Service Managers to make better use of metrics this template offers both a structure to build your metric and a checklist of principles which make it effective. As you complete the template consider the guidance provided in italics (feel free to delete them once used) – you may not have to answer all of them and there may be other detail you wish to add. Review the checklist – this offers criteria which may further your thinking. Your completed template will provide you with a record that you can review regularly to ensure the metric remains useful. Elements of it can be shared with stakeholders to support engagement and provide assurance. You can modify this template or insert it into other documents as required.

Completing this template also offers a means to share your metric in such a way that others can learn from it and consider adaptation or adoption in their own setting. It has been tested by the Metrics Task and Finish group. A shared collection of metrics will be created from your submissions at http://kfh.libraryservices.nhs.uk/metrics-bank/.

This template was informed by a model prepared by Grand River Hospital who have agreed our use. The principles for good metrics were developed by the Metrics Task and Finish group in their Principles for Metrics Report.

Metric definition:
LQAF compliance percentage

Why is it important?
Evidence-based service development
Support stakeholder targets
National data collection and target
Recognised by Trusts as part of LDA requirements
Broad-based picture of quality across multiple service aspects

Process for compiling the Metric:
LQAF Standards Assessment Tool
Completion of LQAF SAT provides score
May be subject to moderation

What does it mean?
Compare performance over time
Potential to benchmark against equivalent
organisations (level of compliance and means of
achieving it)
Discussion with stakeholders about areas of
importance to them within the wider compliance

Desired outcomes:
Useful conversations with
stakeholders
90% compliance for LDA
requirements

Limitations:
− detail can be lost in focus on headline figure
− variation in assessment models limits
  benchmarking

Improvement plans:
Relates to each statement

Reporting:
Annual collection by HEE LKS due around September for London Health
Libraries. South London wide sharing in early September. LQAF compliance
included in annual report and discussed at Library User Boards

CHECKLIST

Does your metric meet the following criteria?

✓   *Meaningful* – does the metric relate to the goals of the organisation, to the needs
     of the users and is it re-examined over time for continuing appropriateness? Do
     other people care about it? Combining two facets can strengthen a metric – for
     example usage by a particular staff group.

✓ *Actionable* – is the metric in areas that the LKS can influence? Does it drive a change in behaviour? The reasons for changes to a metric should be investigated not assumed. Beware self-imposed targets – are they meaningful to stakeholders?

✓ *Reproducible* – the metric is a piece of research so should be clearly defined in advance of use and transparent. It should be able to be replicated over time and constructed with the most robust data available. Collection of data for the metric should not be burdensome to allow repetition when required.

✓ *Comparable* – the metric can be used to see change in the LKS over time. Be cautious if trying to benchmark externally. The diversity of services must be respected – no one metric fits all.

Library and
Knowledge Services

NHS
Health Education England

NHS, TEMPLATE TO SUPPORT THE CREATION AND SHARING OF QUALITY METRICS: OPENATHENS

The construction of metrics is not a straightforward task. There are many aspects of our services that we can collect data on but not all of these are suitable to be metrics. What works for one situation or stakeholder may not be effective for another. Collection should not be potentially inconsistent or excessively burdensome. We need to be able to influence the future scores through our development and delivery of the service.

To help Library & Knowledge Service Managers to make better use of metrics this template offers both a structure to build your metric and a checklist of principles which make it effective. As you complete the template consider the guidance provided in italics (feel free to delete them once used) – you may not have to answer all of them and there may be other detail you wish to add. Review the checklist – this offers criteria which may further your thinking. Your completed template will provide you with a record that you can review regularly to ensure the metric remains useful. Elements of it can be shared with stakeholders to support engagement and provide assurance. You can modify this template or insert it into other documents as required.

Completing this template also offers a means to share your metric in such a way that others can learn from it and consider adaptation or adoption in their own setting. It has been tested by the Metrics Task and Finish group. A shared collection of metrics will be created from your submissions at http://kfh.libraryservices.nhs.uk/metrics-bank/.

This template was informed by a model prepared by Grand River Hospital who have agreed our use. The principles for good metrics were developed by the Metrics Task and Finish group in their Principles for Metrics Report.

Metric definition:

Number of active users on OpenAthens in a given period

Why is it important?

Relates to LQUAF – 1.2d Customer activity/1.2e Service development informed by evidence/1.3c Positive impact (minor)

Can show users are aware and engaged with services

Shows meaningful activity to funders

Simple to collect in an area of high investment so demonstrate value for money for electronic resources

Active users show breadth of engagement. Usage data counts in OpenAthens can be quite variable and feel less reliable than 'has someone used something in a time period or not'

Process for compiling the Metric:

Generate report for required period via OpenAthens Admin > Statistics > generate reports > select Option 1 'List of all usernames/UIDs at this level' > select start and end date

Download report to Excel > drag usernames in Col A and check count

What does it mean?	*Desired outcomes*:
Compare performance during different time periods	Increase number of active users versus equivalent periods
– month versus equivalent month in previous years	
– financial year versus previous	
Potential to benchmark against equivalent organisations	

Limitations:

– changing staffing within the Trust
– IP enabled resources not captured

Improvement plans:

Promotional work. Potential to use activity date by resource or user type to target this

Reporting:

Included in Quarterly stats reports to Library User Boards. Included in Annual reports

CHECKLIST

Does your metric meet the following criteria?

✓ *Meaningful* – does the metric relate to the goals of the organisation, to the needs of the users and is it re-examined over time for continuing appropriateness? Do other people care about it? Combining two facets can strengthen a metric – for example usage by a particular staff group.

✓ *Actionable* – is the metric in areas that the LKS can influence? Does it drive a change in behaviour? The reasons for changes to a metric should be investigated not assumed. Beware self-imposed targets – are they meaningful to stakeholders?

✓ *Reproducible* – the metric is a piece of research so should be clearly defined in advance of use and transparent. It should be able to be replicated over time and constructed with the most robust data available. Collection of data for the metric should not be burdensome to allow repetition when required.

✓ *Comparable* – the metric can be used to see change in the LKS over time. Be cautious if trying to benchmark externally. The diversity of services must be respected – no one metric fits all.

BRITISH LIBRARY, EXAMPLE OF STRATEGIC PERFORMANCE DASHBOARD, 2016/17 FROM THE BRITISH LIBRARY

Quarter 3: April 2016 to December 2016

	Performance Year to Date	Forecast End Year Performance	Trend
1. Heritage made digital			
1.1 Save our sounds programme	▦	▦	⬇
1.2 Two centuries of Indian print	▦	▦	➡
1.3 Qatar partnership	▦	▦	➡
1.4 Heritage Digitisation	▦	▦	➡
1.5 Review and redefine our Digitisation Partnerships	▦	▦	➡
2. St. Pancras transformed			
2.1 Phase 1 procurement partner	▦	▦	➡
2.2 Changing spaces	▦	▦	⬆
2.3 Retail, catering, events and membership	▦	▦	⬆
2.4 Alan Turing Institute partnership	▦	▦	➡

Quarter 3: April 2016 to December 2016

	Performance Year to Date	Forecast End Year Performance	Trend
3. Everyone engaged			
3.1 Living Knowledge Network	▮	▮	→
3.2 BL membership	▮	▮	→
3.3 Knowledge Quarter	▮	▮	→
3.4 BL treasures to China	▮	▮	→
3.5 Grow our capacity for independent research	▮	▮	→
3.6 UK and International Culture programme	▮	▮	→
3.7 Expand our commercial audiences	▮	▮	↓
3.8 Develop BIPC national network	▮	▮	→
3.9 Continue to deliver a 'value added' service for entrepreneurs and SMEs	▮	▮	→
4. Boston Spa renewed			
4.1 UK Printed Collections Management Hub at Boston Spa	▮	▮	→
4.2 Define and document an outline business case for a Shared Digital Collections Hub service	▮	▮	↓
4.3 Develop a programme for Boston Spa renewed	▮	▮	→
4.4 Legal Deposit 2017	▮	▮	→
5. Everything available			
5.1 Develop a programme for digital collection and access technical capability	▮	▮	↓
5.2 Deliver enhancements to end-to-end processing of, and access to, born digital content	▮	▮	↓
5.3 Agree a new strategy for purchased acquisitions	▮	▮	→
5.4 Review research services	▮	▮	→
5.5 Define and develop new 'just in time services'	▮	▮	↓
5.6 Develop our online learning offer	▮	▮	→

Quarter 3: April 2016 to December 2016

	Performance Year to Date	Forecast End Year Performance	Trend
6. Enabling strategies			
6.1 Financial			
6.1.1 Deliver our Finance Strategy 2016–2020 through accurate and robust financial management			→
6.1.2 Develop a robust commercial strategy			→
6.2 People			
6.2.1 Ensure the library is a good place to work			→
6.2.2 Shape the library to deliver our strategy within our resources			→
6.2.3 Develop our staff to learn and adapt to change and keep them motivated			→
6.2.4 Recruit skills and knowledge			→
6.3 IT			
6.3.1 Define and deliver the IT strategy for the BL			↑
6.4 Commercial and fundraising			
6.4.1 Increase our fundraising capacity and impact			↓
6.4.2 Increase income from new and improved commercial services			↓
6.5 Operational effectiveness			
6.5.1 Customer engagement			↑
6.5.2 Service levels			↑
6.5.3 Operational efficiencies			→
6.5.4 Review PLR			→

Key
Performance on or above target/deadline
Performance slightly below target/deadline
Performance significantly below target/deadline

EDGE HILL UNIVERSITY, LEARNING SERVICES: KEY PERFORMANCE INDICATORS

Learning Services: Key Performance Indicators

Edge Hill University

Value Statement:
Customer Excellence: Our Product Is High Quality Support and Resources

	Intended Direction	Value 2011/12	Value 2012/13	Value Sought 2013/14
Satisfaction reported by the NSS	↑	4.13	4.19	4.25
Satisfaction reported by the Student Union 1st and 2nd year survey	↑	3.95	4.03	4.1
Learning Services bi-annual customer satisfaction survey	↑	86.2%	n/a	87%
Number of visits to Learning Services libraries (footfall all sites)	↔	557,492	533,486	533,500
Issues of resources at all Learning Services libraries	↔	259,539	231,873	231,900
Section requests for eBooks	↑	2,177,775	1,807,133	2,000,000
Full text eJournal article requests	↑	577,237	643,813	700,000
Percentage of customer telephone calls to Learning Services support line answered at level 1	↔	97.9%	98.49%	98.49%
Number of unique users of the Learning Services website	↑	34,195	32,856	35,000
Number of page views of the Learning Services website	↑	335,228	417,430	430,000
Number of unique page views of the Learning Services wiki	↑	n/k	7627	8500
Percentage of visitors finding the answer within the ASK US knowledge base	↑	n/a	n/a	30%
Percentage of declared SpLD disability 1st year vs receipt of DSA for SpLD	↑	74%	Available April 2014	80%
Number of students in receipt of DSA accessing specialist study skills support	↑	285	213	290
Number of attendees at scheduled Learning Services staff development sessions	↑	n/k	322	420
Number of students attending Learning Services information literacy activities and support (all)	↑	9573	8361	9000

KPI 1:
Learning Services is the go to place for study, support and resources

Value Statement:
Operational Excellence: Our Operational Systems Are Customer Focused and Effective

	Intended Direction	Value 2011/12	Value 2012/13	Value Sought 2013/14
KPI 2: *Learning Edge is a core teaching and learning system*				
Average Learning Edge Bb 9.1 active users (per month)	↑	14,897	13,410	15,000
Average monthly active users of Bb mobile learn app	↑	1266	4221	7000
Percentage uptime/availability of Learning Edge	↑	99.95%	99.99%	100%
Average monthly daily logins to Learning Edge Bb 9.1	↑	2923	3327	3800
Satisfaction recorded within classroom equipment and support survey	↑	n/k	85.71%	90%
Average cost per section request for eBooks	↔	0.04p	0.05p	0.05p
Average cost per fulltext article request for eJournals	↔	0.73p	0.74p	0.74p
KPI 3: *Learning Services provide value for money*				
Issues of resources at all Learning Services libraries	↔	259,539	231,873	231,900
Section requests for eBooks	↑	2,177,775	1,807,133	2,000,000
Full text eJournal article requests	↑	577,237	643,813	700,000
Percentage of readings lists received vs live modules	↑	n/k	51%	60%
£ cost per head for Learning Edge (Bb) technologies	↔	Confidential	Confidential	Confidential

Learning Services: Key Performance Indicators

Edge Hill University

Value Statement:
Staff Engagement: Our Staff Drive Our Customer and Operational Excellence Improvements

	Intended Direction	Value 2011/12	Value 2012/13	Value Sought 2013/14
KPI 4: Staff are proud of the service and willing to go the extra mile				
Percentage of staff rating engagement in a Learning Services staff survey	↑	n/a	tbc	tbc
Average wellbeing and attendance to university average (excluding long-term absence)	↑	Available on request	Available on request	Available on request
Number of staff nominated for student led support awards	↑	n/a	7	9
Percentage of satisfaction with knowledgeable staff recorded by mystery shopper	↑	94%	n/a	95%
Number of Learning Services staff attending internal staff development sessions	↑	97	90	97
KPI 5: Learning Services staff are engaged in academic liaison				
Number of attendees at Learning Services bespoke staff development sessions	↑	n/k	330	360
Attendance at programme and Faculty Boards	↑	n/k	n/k	tbc
Attendance at meetings and one to ones with University colleagues	↑	n/k	n/k	tbc

MCMASTER UNIVERSITY LIBRARY SCORECARD

McMaster University Library Scorecard (21/09/11)

McMaster
University
LIBRARY

	Objectives	Measures	Score	Strategic initiatives*
User perspective	1. Integrate the Library into the University's Teaching, Learning and Research Mission	1.1 New content in institutional repository	◑	Digitization program Institutional repository
		1.2 Research grants	◑	Sherman Ctr. for Digital Scholarship Teaching Commons
		1.3 Library involvement in student learning	◑	Blended Learning Teaching Commons
	2. Improve discovery of and access to scholarly resources	2.1 Collection satisfaction	○	
		2.2 Downloads from the institutional repository	○	Institutional repository
		2.3 Use of licensed E-resources	○	Library web site
		2.4 Objects digitized through vendor contracts	○	Digitization program
	3. Create world-class teaching and learning spaces	3.1 Upgraded classrooms	●	
		3.2 Satisfaction with library spaces	○	Accessibility audit Blended services Good ideas incubator
		3.3 Silent / quiet study seats	○	Transform physical collections
		3.4 Gate count	●	
	4. Strive for exemplary service that is responsive to user needs	4.1 Service satisfaction	○	Accessibility audit Blended services Ron Joyce Centre Good ideas incubator
Internal process	5. Marketing: Promote awareness of the Library's rich collections, state-of-the-art facilities and exemplary services	5.1 Daily news stories	◑	
	6. Track efficiency and effectiveness of Library programs and services	6.1 New monograph use	○	
		6.2 Research collections backlog	○	
Learning and growth	7. Develop highly-trained, technologically-fluent superlative staff	7.1 Committee membership	○	
		7.2 Knowledgeable staff	○	Accessibility audit Staff training plans
		7.3 Training plans	○	Staff training plans
	8. Nurture a healthy, collaborative dynamic work place	8.1 ClimateQUAL	○	Organizational climate Staff training plans
		8.2 Healthy work place in-house survey	○	Staff training plans
	9. Grow an evidence-based culture that encourages innovation and risk taking.	9.1 Assessment plans	○	
Finance	10. Secure appropriate financial resources to maintain a world-class research library	10.1 Total budget allocation	○	
		10.2 Total donations	●	Library development web presence
		10.3 Revenue generation	○	

◑ Meeting target   ○ Approaching target   ● Not meeting target   ○ N/A

INDEX

Note: Page numbers followed by *f* indicate figures *t* indicate tables and *b* indicate boxes.